AF843475

# imagine 03 –
# PERFORMANCE DRIVEN ENVELOPES

Delft University of Technology, Faculty of Architecture,
Chair of Design of Constructions

# imagine 03

SERIES EDITED BY
Ulrich Knaack
Tillmann Klein
Marcel Bilow

This book is made possible by the support of the following partners:

PENNSTATE imagine structure imagine envelope

# PERFORMANCE DRIVEN ENVELOPES

Ulrich Knaack
Tillmann Klein
Marcel Bilow
Holger Techen

010 Publishers, Rotterdam 2011

1.
2.
3.
4.
5.

# CONTENTS

# 1. INTRODUCTION

To many of us, the first things that come to mind when thinking of performance are racing cars. And to those with less gas running through their veins it might at least be associated with speed, competition, reaching limits or other extreme activities. Performance is linked to a goal, and to some extent, it is measurable. High performance in one area often suppresses other functions. The Formula 1 car, for example, is built to win in its racing category, but will score very badly when used for holiday vacations. Performance in a more general sense can be described by the level that a targeted requirement is fulfilled.

Most products are designed to satisfy many functions. A standard car must not only transport people and goods, it should perform that task in a comfortable manner and with a minimum amount of gas. At the same time, emotional values must be addressed to convince a potential buyer. Multi functionality always bears the risk of conflicting requirements. A comfortable ride asks for a large and heavy car which generally has a negative influence on gas consumption.

The same is true for building envelopes. A multitude of requirements have to be addressed. At some point the need for efficient sun shading will conflict with the demand for daylighting and visual contact with the outside world. Natural ventilation will lead to undesired energy losses in winter and so forth. Therefore, it is very difficult to fundamentally improve the performance of the building envelope simply because of its complexity.

A strategy around this problem is to examine all the different problems individually. This strategy of course does not guarantee success, but it helps to analyze and rethink the core requirements that the performance of building envelopes should be focused on.
It is uncompromised performance-oriented design that stirs our imagination. If the boundaries of the possible are touched upon, we are inspired to overcome the limits of our own material environment.
Here are some examples:

## WORKING EFFICIENCY: WINDMILLS

The Dutch windmill was primarily used to pump water from the polders; it became a crucial element in creating the unique Dutch landscape.
At the time of its first appearance it represented the latest technologies.
The wings covered with reefing sails catch the wind to generate electricity.
Numerous examples are still functional today, removed from their original

purpose; but valuable as reminders of the cultural past. The contemporary counterparts of the windmill – the wind turbines – have mast heights up to 150 m and generate enough energy for thousands of households. The primary purpose of harvesting energy has remained the same. Aerodynamically optimized wings, as long as a soccer field, rely on the latest material technologies. No one really enjoys living in their close proximity; but again, they are symbols for a sustainable future. To many, their beauty lies in their symbolic value and the uncompromised design of efficiency.

## ARTISTIC PERFORMANCE: RED BLUE CHAIR

Gerrit Rietveld´s idea about comfort was rather rational, and had to do with being attentive and thinking about one's environment rather than the physical comfort that goes along with relaxation. In this sense, the success of this chair is related to a highly artistic performance and its representation of the concept of the De Stijl movement.

## PUSHING THE LIMITS: RACING YACHTS

Until the 20th century, yacht design was typically viewed as an intuitive art. Later, competitive sailing led to scientific methods to understand the connection of sail performance to hull shape and sail plan. At some point, handicapping rules needed to be implemented to provide mechanisms for different yacht types to compete, with the most skillful sailor winning. These rules would typically describe sail area, boat length, weight, etc., and subject them to complex formulas. Exploring the limits leads to designs that focus on pushing them further and further. In turn, the new designs – based on new technologies – lead to an adaptation of the rules. Over decades and centuries, racing yachts have developed in an incremental process. Yacht performance is thus measured by its success in accordance with the limiting rules.

## CHANGING PERFORMANCE GOALS: SENZ° STORM UMBRELLA

We expect a good umbrella to protect us from rain. We also expect it to be round, which might be a result of its beautiful rotation symmetrical folding structure. We are also used to the fact that its lightweight construction renders it unusable in strong winds. Perhaps it is not surprising that this product was invented in the wind beaten Netherlands. The senz° umbrella exploits a simple trick: by giving it a direction, structural stability and wind resistance were improved to make it stand up to 10 Beaufort. The shape might not provide as much protection against rain as the round standard umbrella, but it claims a unique market position. A small amount of performance in one area was sacrificed to gain new performance in another. It seems as if before the senz° umbrella, no one questioned the performance goals of umbrellas.

1 Historic windmill at Kinderdijk
2 Modern wind turbines can generate energy for thousands of households
3 The Red Blue Chair by Gerrit Rietveld

4

5

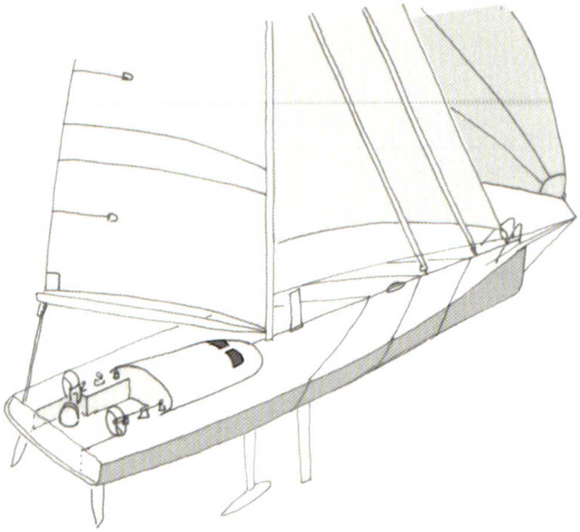

6

7

8

9

4 The Yacht Valkyrie 1893. In her racing class, water length was virtually the only criterion subject to limitations. This led to large overhangs and ridiculously oversized sail areas.
5 Modern racing yachts such as this IMOCA Open 60 have flat bottoms, broad sterns and deep blade-like keels. They are not much more than large surfboards
6 Changing performance goals: senz° storm umbrella
7 Changing performance goals: senz° storm umbrella
8 Bread bag clip and strip: cost as a driving factor
9 Space Shuttle Atlantis takes flight. Credit: NASA

## COST AS A DRIVING FACTOR: THE BREAD BAG CLIP

The bread bag clip is a rarely acknowledged everyday device. Its primary function is to close a bread bag in a reversible manner. Its predecessor was a flexible strip composed of two wires, connected by a plastic band. The bread clip is constructed of a single material that deflects to open and then returns to its original shape. It is strong enough to perform this shape change repeatedly until the bag is emptied. The shape is designed to grip onto the plastic bag when closed and prevent the clip from sliding off.
Its market success depends on one outstanding characteristic: being ultimately cheap while providing the same functionality as its competitors. Later versions even have the expiration date imprinted: a truly multifunctional device.

## LIGHTNESS AS A GOAL: ASTRONAUTICS

It requires a large amount of energy and is outrageously expensive to transport just one kilogram of material into space. These facts justify all measures to reduce weight. Space programs have taken credit for the development of lightweight structures, heat resistance and insulation materials. But NASA also introduced a process strategy to build their spacecrafts. It was simply impossible to solve this tremendously complex task in one singular approach. The different tasks, such as computing technology for controls, hull design, landing gear or space suits, were distributed to different teams. Each team had its own budget and focused solely on one specific problem. A separate team monitored the process and was responsible for the integration of the individual developments.

Fortunately, buildings do not have to fly into space; but with this book we would like to inspire you to try it – well, not literally; but with reference to the performance issues of building envelopes. Usability, comfort, security, sustainability and material aspects are such issues, and will be explained later in the book.

Performance Driven Envelopes is part of the "Imagine" book series, initiated by the Faculty of Architecture at the TU Delft, chair of Design of Constructions, Prof. Dr. Ulrich Knaack. Each book of the series focuses on a specific aspect within the field of building technology. As the title implies, the series comprises a collection of ideas and concepts, but also elaborated design studies – all aimed at further exploring the field of research.
Its main purpose is to inspire the reader to take on and continue the work.

# 2. A ROADMAP FOR THE BUILDING ENVELOPE

# A ROADMAP FOR THE BUILDING ENVELOPE

Which topics currently concern us when conceptualizing and developing new façades? Where do these topics come from, and what topics will evolve over the next few years? And how can we think ahead to develop the topics of the future? This contribution provides a short overview of the current state of affairs. It introduces trends and tries to derive possible developments – a roadmap for the building envelope, fall 2011. However, the purpose is not to offer concrete solutions, but rather to recognize tendencies and principal directions that we can pursue for the coming years; as designers, engineers and/or researchers.

## FAÇADE – THE CURRENT STATUS

When talking about the building envelope, we typically differentiate between load-bearing wall and façade. The former involves applying additional layers to the interior and exterior surfaces to increase the comfort performance, meaning the performance capability in terms of insulating, sealing and surface finishing. The most common type of closed façades are skeletal systems, consisting of a load-bearing frame clad with complete wall panels or individual layers that serve different functions. Post-beam façades – the most akin to the previously mentioned skeletal systems – and element façades have established themselves as the main façade types for large areas of transparency. With element façades, the façade elements are completely premanufactured and need only be mounted into position on site.

Naturally, there are numerous other systems and alternative solutions: for example, prefabrication of entire walls for prefab housing. The prefabrication process includes plastering and full finishing. Or large, so-called mega-units that support faster building times depending on the transportation capacity and logistics. However, these are specialized solutions that in spite of their benefits do not account for the majority of projects.

In this book, the performance of the façade is divided into the following areas: usability (aesthetics, design, user functions), comfort (air, noise, radiation, temperature, humidity), safety (physical stress, fire, contamination, destruction), sustainability (durability, energy), and material (production, material properties and assembly). These groupings allow us to devise development potential. And they highlight that the façade as the building envelope must not only fulfill purely technical requirements such as insulating and sealing; but must also meet more general functional demands such as safety, functionality and design. And sustainability is, of course, an important aspect because it is the one criterion to determine sensible energy consumption.

Understanding the building envelope as a factor of the overall building performance has significantly changed how we perceive and deal with walls and façades, since they are no longer considered passive elements that provide protection based only on the material. Rather, building envelopes are adaptive systems that respond to changing conditions in a daily, seasonal or even life cycle. They can even be designed as active systems that support the actual operation of the building by generating and thus providing energy.

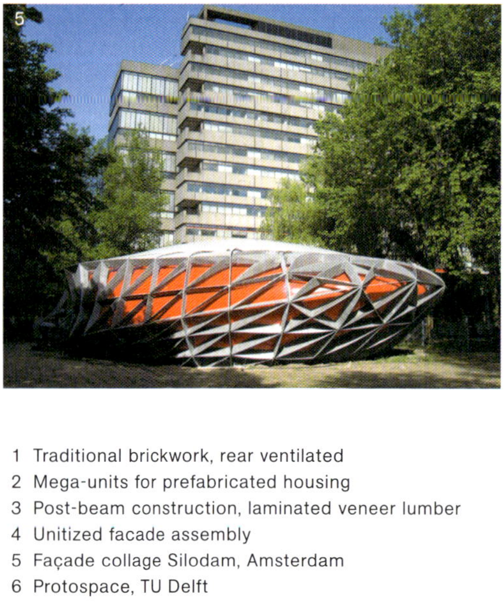


1 Traditional brickwork, rear ventilated
2 Mega-units for prefabricated housing
3 Post-beam construction, laminated veneer lumber
4 Unitized facade assembly
5 Façade collage Silodam, Amsterdam
6 Protospace, TU Delft

Besides functionality, cost is a factor that cannot be neglected, particularly since the cost of façades and roofs of Western standard, depending on the surface finish, accounts for +/- 25% of the construction cost of a building. Looking at other subcontracts, the shell of the building, for example, shows that the developments in the building industry including materials, manufacturing and construction methods and the resulting cost (+/- 20% of the overall cost) have evolved over a very long time, whereas significant developmental steps of the building envelope have taken place during only the past 100 years.

Another critical factor is appearance – it need not be mentioned that the building envelope is the one building part that has significant influence on the architectural design. Rather, the question as to how far architectural trends impact the development of the building envelope – technological as well as aesthetic – serves as a basis for discussion for possible new developments. The influence of the trend "Form Follows Energy" can be seen in current projects which are described later in this book.

The influence of the trend "Fuck the Content" is less distinct even though it should have a much greater impact on the exterior design.

"Form fucks Function" follows a similar direction because it also gives preference to aesthetics over functionality. It has to be said though, that these last two trends resemble the swing of a pendulum, opposing the tendencies of structuralism and technological focus – and a pendulum will eventually swing back.

In order to describe the current state of discussion of the development of the building envelope, we have isolated some developmental trends and will describe them in the following pages.

## TREND TOWARD FULLY GLAZED CONSTRUCTIONS

This topic has evolved from the desire for maximum transparency; to create an alternative to the massive, enclosed buildings of the 1970s and 1980s.
The first step was story-high glazing to achieve maximum transparency with minimal substructures. In a second step, improved glazing qualities and larger pane dimensions let this technology evolve into multi-story façades that consisted of less and less load-bearing components and therefore transferred the load-bearing function onto the glass. Responsible for these developments were improvements in glass quality such as tempered safety glass (heat-strengthened glass), annealed glass (also heat-strengthened but with a larger break pattern), and laminated safety glass (two or more layers of glass bonded together), as well as an improvement of the mounting technology by using flush point fixtures. Subsequently, the evolution of the load-bearing structure to pre-tensioned structures, planar cable-net structures, and glass-only load-bearing constructions further influenced this development.

According to the cycle that architectural trends typically undergo, fully glazed constructions have passed their peak; however, the technologies that evolved from this trend are part of today's architectural repertoire and are implemented when needed.

## DOUBLE FAÇADE

As a predecessor of modern high-tech architecture, double façades evolved in the 1950s. At that time, early pioneers examined methods to gain energy, for example with collector façades. Here, the air between a massive wall and an exterior glass pane is warmed by solar radiation and can be fed into the room as desired.

7

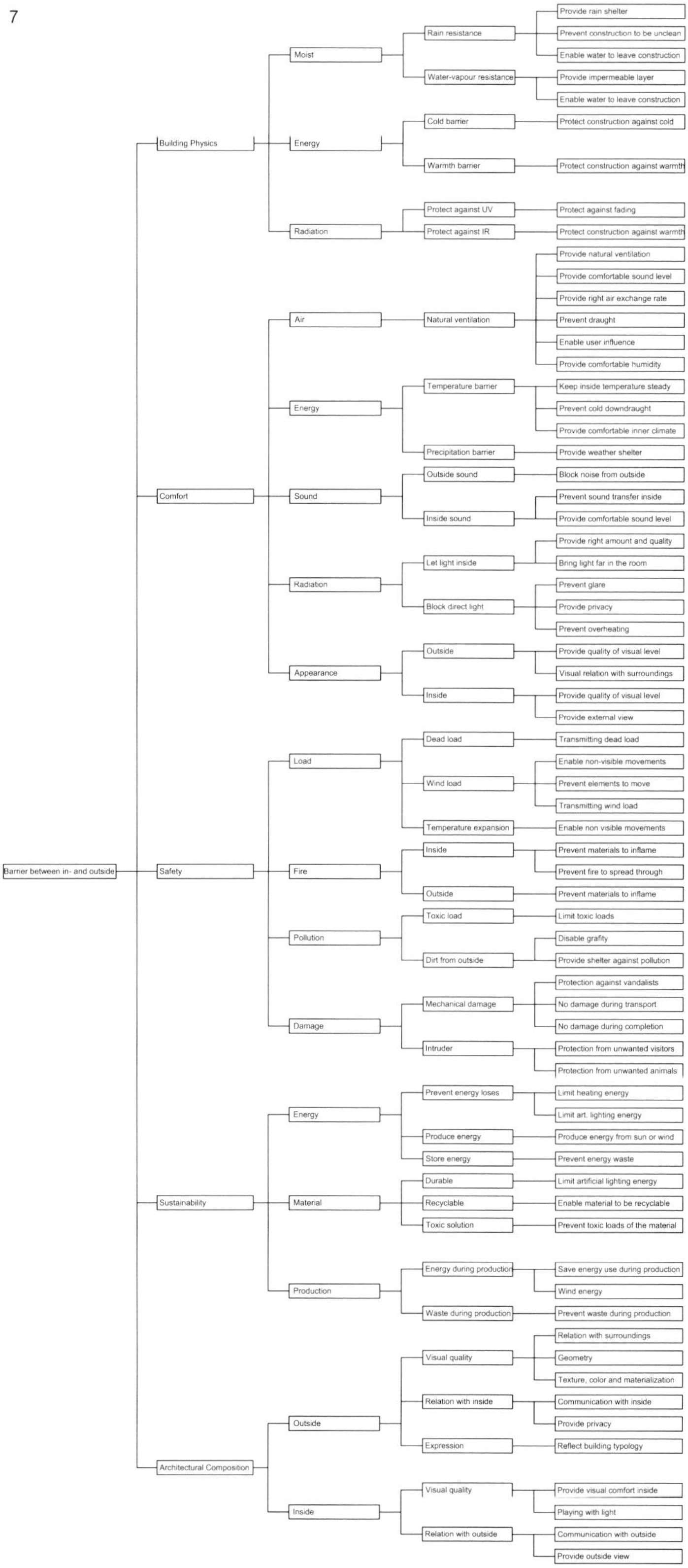


7 Façade function tree

In the 1990s, this topic generated a series of different types of double façades. They can be differentiated by the principles used: exhaust façade – the exhaust indoor air is sucked out of the room through the space between the glass panels so that thermal energy cannot penetrate the façade from the outside to the inside; second-skin façade, corridor façade, box-window façade and shaft-box façade. As the name implies, a second-skin façade includes a second façade layer – typically made of glass – that provides additional protection for the building, but also creates more thermal energy which needs to be regulated. The corridor façade also includes a second glass layer; but here horizontal divisions on story-level offer increased control options. Additional vertical divisions provide even more controllability in the box-window façade. And the shaft-box façade allows additional regulation of the energy flow through a vertical exhaust shaft in the façade.

Even though double façades have definitely reached or passed their peak, and are scarcely used in new buildings, we should not understand this development as the end of the technology, but rather recognize that the knowledge and technology gained from these façade evolutions is like a gene pool that we can draw from to apply the technology appropriately and sensibly in terms of technical as well as formative aspects.

## COMPONENT FAÇADE

Component façades should be understood as the logical development from double façades: in part, double façades already were an integrative element of a building's building services system; so the logical consequence was to add even more functionality. In addition to a few other examples, the Post Tower in Bonn, Germany, is usually regarded as the start of this development even though individual components were still installed into the façade and close-by floor areas in separate steps, whereas for later projects the components were premanufactured as modules to be integrated into façade elements.

The potential of this approach lies in the possibility of complete function integration, premanufacturing for later on-site installation, and the possibility to design a more flexible building by freeing it from building services installations. The difficulties of this approach are the logistics and the fact that two previously completely separate building sectors are forced to not only coordinate but also to ensure common quality and cost levels; meaning we can definitely expect significant developmental leaps in this area.

## FREE-FORM

With the introduction of digital planning and the evolution of appropriate tools, an architectural style has developed that follows a new creative approach by trying to annihilate known shapes. The two most prominent tendencies are, firstly, to realize a particular form or shape using the computer as a planning aid, and secondly to base a design on defined parameters, which the computer uses to generate the design.

For both trends, the computer is the means to illustrate the design and to make it realizable as an integrated part of the production process. This means, that not only the performance capability of hardware and software are critical, but also an interface with the production process. The latter provides the link to actually built architecture but it also raises difficulties: rendering free-formed architecture on the computer does not mean it can be easily realized. Solutions are created either on a purely technical level (shingles, plaster, etc.) or as the result of skeletonizing the structure into manageable components, which meant that new production technologies were developed in addition to digital process chains.

Since this process does not yet yield good results for all areas of construction and surface finishing materials, we can expect more in-depth research.

## ENERGY

Naturally, energy is one of the most important topic of façade discussion today: the tendencies to consider the building envelope as a significant factor for regulating the energy necessary to operate a building are obvious – the influence of the façade on the overall performance seems logical. Previously described topics such as the double façade and component façade prove this tendency as do ever more sophisticated evaluation tools that allow us to apply energy values for overall evaluation depending on the geographic orientation of the building and the façade materials used.

Simultaneously, a trend is developing to include embedded energy values – energy needed to produce the materials and components used – into the overall energy evaluation of the planning process. If we isolate this trend from the much more complex overall evaluation of a building or even an entire location, possibilities evolve to examine different façade-related developmental directions, in order to identify extreme solutions related to the amounts of energy needed for production (super-light versus massive façades, dismountable component façades to composites made from one material).

## ADAPTABILITY

In a broader sense, double and component façades are the predecessors of adaptive façades because they support the functions of a building and can adapt accordingly. These factors are supplemented by controlling transparency levels and the outer appearance of the façade. Initial examples with LED's have attracted great attention and thus driven the success of this technology integrated into façades. Therefore, today, large LED displays not only serve the function of advertising but also change the appearance of entire buildings.

However, since the application of this technology involves great cost and its aggressive, dynamic appearance dominates the surroundings, it is mostly applied to isolated projects. But we can still expect large potential from LED technologies, particularly if they are integrated into common materials such as glass, metal, concrete, etc. And the possibility of very accurately controlling the brightness to influence transparency levels from the inside to the outside and vice versa, promises possibilities beyond those of mere advertising.

## SURFACES / TEXTURES

Naturally, surfaces and textures have always been an important design tool in architecture – but even so; contemporary architecture and its façades are showing a definite trend toward extroverted surface design. Concrete surfaces are modified by adding textures to the formwork, materials are used in unusual contexts, and the use of very large elements or filigree components in large repetitions create new façade designs. Besides such formative play with materials and forms to identify entirely new imageries, another trend could be to integrate other topics into the surface areas: can additional building functions

8

9

10

11

12

13

8 Parc de la Villette, Paris
9 Apple Store, New York
10 Corridor façade, Düsseldorf
11 Shaft-box façade, ARAG – Düsseldorf
12 Component façade, Post Tower, Bonn
13 Component façade, Capricorn, Düsseldorf

be integrated into the building envelope? And how do they change the façade or even its changeability? These questions lead us to the topic of material development.

## MATERIALS AND PRODUCTION

The field of materials is currently undergoing a true hype! Besides in architecture, it is most reflected by the development of new professions (material scout, for example) and the great number of material libraries and online services, all focused on offering ever new material solutions or driving innovation by employing materials in an unusual context.

It is interesting to see that the use of certain materials in architecture also undergoes cycles; on one hand this is due to the developments in architecture itself, on the other it has to do with marketing activities and technological material development. There was the previously described trend to build with glass; now, however, we can see a development drive in the field of concrete. In addition to well organized marketing activities on international level there are also technological developments – "light-transmissive" concrete, "heat-insulating" concrete, amongst others, more about this later in this book – that are used in "new" architectural projects. The same is true for the material wood: in addition to the known products, wood composites consisting of layered wood-based materials and even extruded wood profiles are now available on the market.

Another highly interesting area is that of plastic composites. Besides great technological steps (processing, strengths, combinations), an important development related to ecological tolerability (components, recycling, composting) has taken place; only the fire prevention issue, always a deciding factor in the building industry, has yet to be solved.

## MARKETS

When dealing with the topic building envelope, we also need to monitor the market with all its facets and players: there is a trend toward bundling different technologies to create "general façade contractors", in addition to the known players including raw material processors, semi-manufactured part suppliers and construction companies. As a further logical consequence we can expect that building services and façade, which together define the performance of the building envelope, will be handled by new consortia who offer this performance as an integral component of the building. Thus, a new type of general contractor will emerge, controlling a much larger share of the budget than does the traditional general contractor who typically comes from shell construction.

Another market aspect is the fact that due to its world-leading market position, the European façade industry and its largest players in particular are very export oriented. On the other hand, the industry is under pressure because labor cost still accounts for a large share of the overall cost, which furthers low labor cost countries with sufficient technological knowledge to push into this attractive market.

But besides these "normal' market processes, the building industry is particular in that market leaders in the area of engineering and production understand unique architectural ideas as a stimulus to realize designs that hitherto could not have been built. Creating customized solutions for seemingly unrealizable design ideas not only promotes innovation but also strengthens a company's market position.

## OPEN QUESTIONS: NOW WHAT?

What are the questions that still need answering? It is impossible to compile

14 Guggenheim Museum, Bilbao
15 Walt Disney Concert Hall, Los Angeles
16 Walt Disney Concert Hall, Los Angeles
17 Times Square, New York
18 Lafayette, Peking

an all-encompassing list, but we can isolate individual issues for which we can develop scenarios or even technical or product solutions. To organize them in this book, we use the previously described division into the following areas of performance: usability (aesthetics, design, user functions), comfort (air, noise, radiation, temperature, humidity), safety (physical stress, fire, contamination, destruction), sustainability (durability, energy), and material (production, material properties and assembly). By means of this performance categorization, different façade solutions are introduced as principles. They will aid designers and constructors in understanding the subject matter.

The advantage of this approach is that a topic can be efficiently examined studying one or more of the solutions presented in the category. It also allows us to temporarily ignore problems with other functions, technical solutions or creative demands.
However, this kind of temporary single-mindedness also has disadvantages: design, construction and architecture need to be seen globally – everything affects everything else. Therefore: single-minded solutions are well suited to reach the root of the matter, but can only fail in actual application. Thus, a book dealing with performance driven envelopes must, in conclusion, explore the topic of integration since maximum integration is the ultimate goal for integral principles.

19 Amsterdam School
20 Library, Utrecht
21 Material collage, Marcel Bilow
22 Concrete profile, Durapcat Hahn
23 Design School Essen, façade includes active thermal insulation

# 3. THE WAY WE WORK

Workshop Delft School of Design (DSD) at the Faculty of Architecture

# THE WAY WE WORK

It takes two things to find the needle in the haystack: firstly, the absolute belief in being able to find it, and secondly, to simply start looking. In fact, there are many needles to be found – as many as there are possible innovations in the field of building envelopes.

Besides believing and the hands-on approach, there is strategy. We focus on a particular topic, such as Deflateables, Rapids or Energy covered in the previous volumes of this Imagine book series, and share our passion with the network of our friends. Working together in organized events propels one's imagination. A combination of professionals and students is very inspiring, and very often proves to be the right mixture to create the free and inventive environment we desire. We thrive for an open process, which primarily means that any idea is welcome and none are rejected. It is like throwing a stone and seeing where it lands. It might take a few throws but eventually there will be a hit! In a next step, the ideas are developed further. The results are reflected by the 'principles' presented in this book. Some remain rather general, whereas others might reach an in-depth or even realistic level. The network idea includes that everyone is encouraged to do the same: pick up the ideas and develop them further. The final goal is to create an imaginary approach from which we can all benefit.

It took several years to develop the content for this book; many people were involved in various events from which we drew ideas:

In 2008, **Delft School of Design (DSD)** at the Faculty of Architecture organized three workshops with students under Bige Tuncer. The following guest lecturers were invited: Klaus Daniels / Emeritus ETH Zurich, Werner Sobek / University of Stuttgart, ILEK, Neil Thomas / Atelier One, Thomas Auer / Transsolar, Stuttgart and Holger Techen / University of Applied Sciences, Frankfurt.

In 2009, **imagine structure** organized a professional workshop in the heart of Frankfurt's old town with the following participants:
Heiko Weissbach / Sauerbruch Hutton, Kari Silloway / KSP Engel und Zimmermann Architekten, Sabine Einhäuser / Hahlbrock GmbH, Johannes Fokken and Andre Glück / Fischer Architekten GmbH, Lutz Langer / kadawittfeldarchitektur, Oliver and Svantje Kühn, GKK Architekten, Christian Heuchel / Ortner&Ortner, Anna Gerlach / Benthem Crouwel GmbH, Martin Haas / Behnisch Architekten, Margit Pfundstein / BASF, Claudia Lüling / University of Applied Sciences Frankfurt, Stefan Hauser / Ducon, Max Weber / Hausgemacht Architekten, Friedrich Dassler / XIA, Holger Techen, Matthias Michel, Arne Kuenstler and Martin Manegold / imagine structure, Thomas Auer and Matthias Rudolph / Transsolar, Tillman Klein, Marcel Bilow and Ulrich Knaack / imagine envelope

In 2011, **Penn State University** hosted a student workshop at the Faculty of Architecture in collaboration with TU Delft. The PSU teachers in attendance were Scott Wing, Ute Poerschke and Katsu Muramoto. The workshop was sponsored by the Eleanor R. Stuckemann Visiting Chair.

In addition, students participating in the Façade Master Programs of the **Hochschule Ostwestfalen Lippe** and the **Delft University of Technology** have focused on contributing to this publication.

We would like to apologize for not being able to name every single participant individually. The sheer number of students involved makes this an impossible task. However, their names are attached to the different contributions they have made in the form of 'principles'.

We would like to thank our sponsors and supporters who were crucial for the development of the content of this book:

**Delft University of Technology**, Faculty of Architecture, Netherlands
**Penn State University**, Faculty of Architecture, Eleanor R. Stuckemann Visiting Chair, University Park, USA
**Royal Danish Academy of Fine Arts – School of Architecture**, Copenhagen, Denmark
**Transsolar Climate Engineering**, Stuttgart, Germany
**Imagine Structure** – Structural Design, Frankfurt, Germany
**Imagine Envelope** – Façade Consulting, The Hague, Netherlands

Ulrich Knaack, Marcel Bilow, Tillmann Klein

Workshop imagine structure / DSD Workshop

Workshop impressions

# 4. PERFORMANCE PRINCIPLES

# 4.0. INTRODUCTION

One typical instrument of the imagine book series is the quick sketching of ideas; for documentation and to make them accessible to designers and constructors as a source of inspiration. The principles collected in this book are organized in the following categories: usability (aesthetics, design, user functions), comfort (air, noise, radiation, temperature, humidity), safety (physical stress, fire, contamination, destruction), sustainability (durability, energy), and material (production, material properties and assembly). In addition to the keywords used in all previous imagine publications, we defined a performance focus for each principle in this volume.

# 4.1. USABILITY

Usability describes the formative design of the façade, its integration into the urban environment, the aesthetic and creative impression of the building. Also covered in this section is the haptic experience of the building envelope – exterior and interior – as well as aspects of user-related functions such as opening and closing, controlled transparency or opaqueness, and individualization of the building envelope.

# CURTAIN WALL 2050

28-04-2009

IMAGINED BY Thiemo Ebbert
KEYWORDS mono-material, self-organizing, load-bearing, futuristic
PERFORMANCE accessibility

Modern materials can change their physical properties upon the application of electric energy. The construction material of this wall is solid and load-bearing when in a passive state. When it is activated, the material softens and contracts. Thus, the wall opens by itself.

This effect is not restricted to a specific area of the wall, but can occur in any desired location. Thus, anyone could cross through the wall and produce their individual curtain wherever needed. If the user is equipped with a RFID chip, individual access can be granted when approaching the building. Unauthorized people would be confronted with a solid wall.

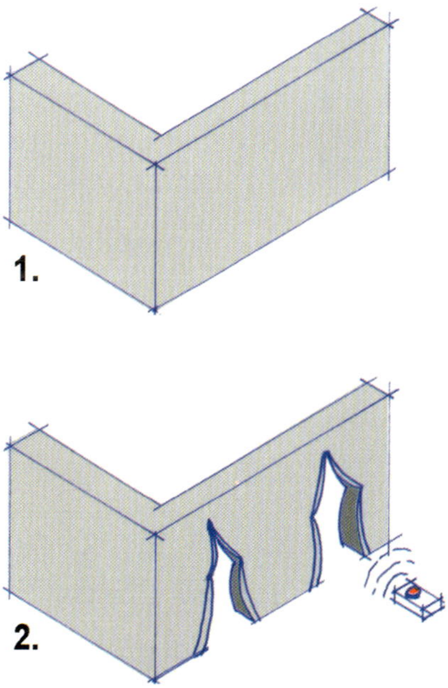

# DIALOGUE/DISPLAY

09-04-2011

**IMAGINED BY** Miriam Lott, guided by U. Knaack, T. Klein and M. Bilow
Part of the Future Envelope class at Penn State University
**KEYWORDS** flexible paper, display, moving elements, façade
**PERFORMANCE** accessibility

This façade works as both a drawing surface and a display system for artwork. In its simplest form, paper scrolls through a system of rollers transferring images from the interior drawing space to the exterior community face.

In order to transform a paper system into a weatherproof and self-supporting façade, more layers must be added. The tubes of the rollers serve as the main structure with the other elements being threaded onto the system, such as cross bracing and glass connectors. This design aims at exposing the system as a learning tool. Therefore, simple gear systems connect and turn the rollers, powered by a manual hand crank.

The translucent properties of the paper allow the system to effectively work as a shading system for the highly glazed nature of a display façade. While the lower units of the system are blank drawing surfaces, the upper units will use a moiré-type effect to display pre-determined works of art. Dividing the art into alternating circles that form and blur the image as the façade scrolls brings a simple glass façade to life.

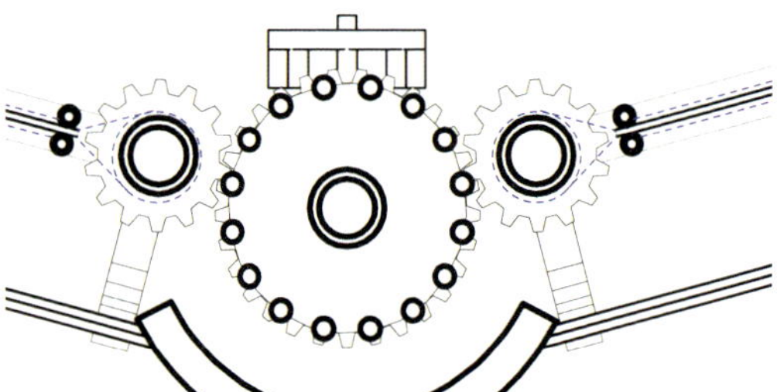

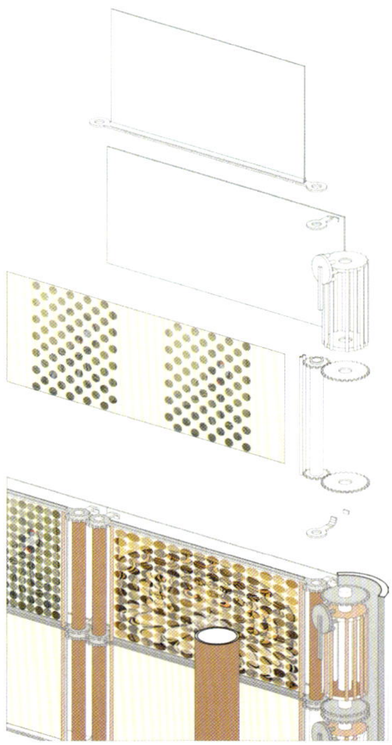

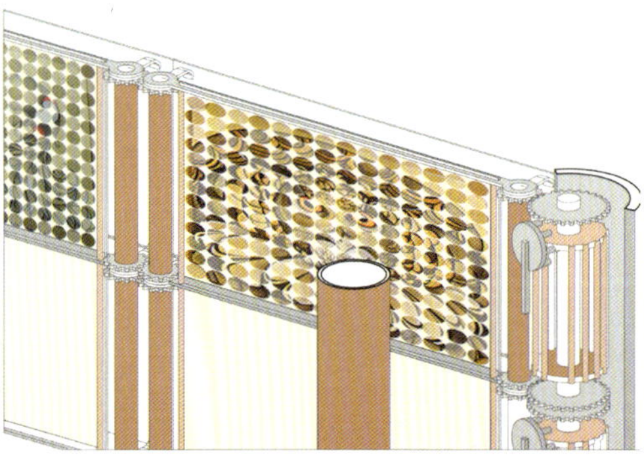

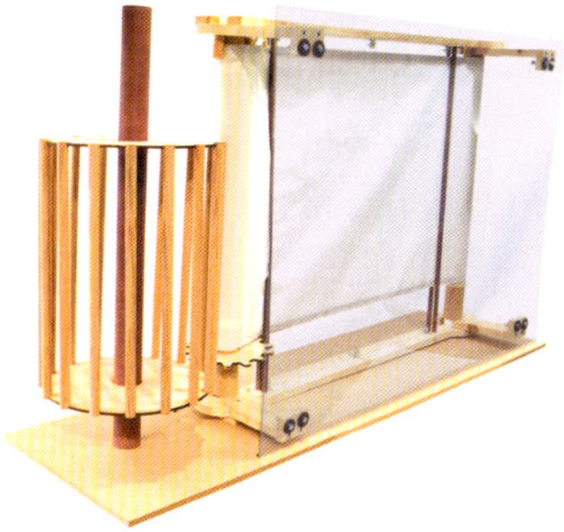

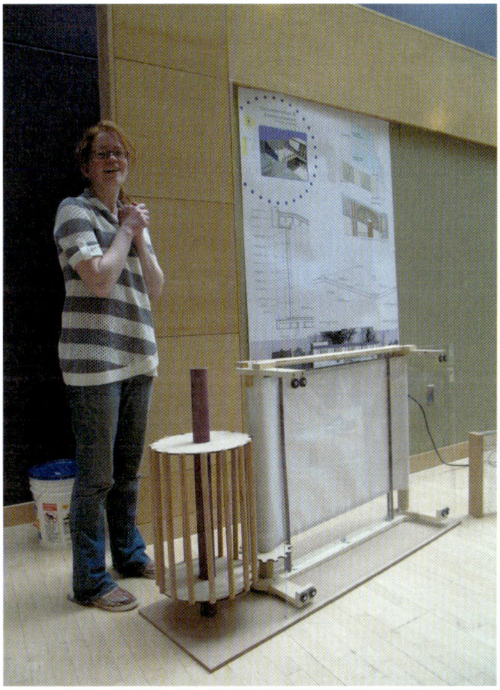

# DUG-IN DUCT

28-04-2009

**IMAGINED BY** Thiemo Ebbert
**KEYWORDS** mono-material, free-form, adapting, interior
**PERFORMANCE** accessibility

Contemporary interior design favors plain and solid, homogenous walls. And typical facility management prefers to have easy access to all installation ducts in order to replace, add, or maintain components. Adaptable materials can solve both problems.

The wall coating is made of an adaptable material. In a passive state, it forms a homogenous, solid surface. When activated, the material softens and can be reshaped by hand. Thus, if someone needs access to the installation ducts, they activate the wall coating and dig into the installation space. When all work is done, the coating is straightened again and changed to its passive state. The wall returns to its original appearance.

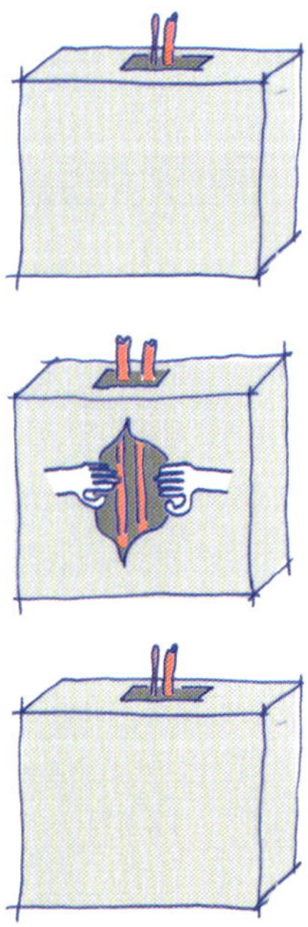

1.

2.

3.

# FREE-FORM SPACE

20-03-2003

**IMAGINED BY** GKK Architekten Berlin
**KEYWORDS** structure, concrete, free-form space
**PERFORMANCE** free-form

This project was designed in the course of a competition submission for the design and remodelling of a former factory building into a museum for medical technology. The new building, which connects all former building parts, was developed as a free-formed concrete structure. The floor slabs curve into columns, which in turn melt into the ceilings. This creates a continuous spatial arrangement that comprises load-bearing structure and interior space. The façade assimilates the overall structure and mimics it with a microstructure.

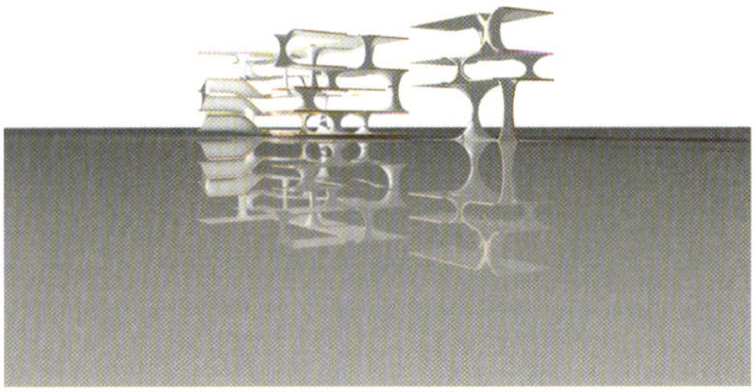

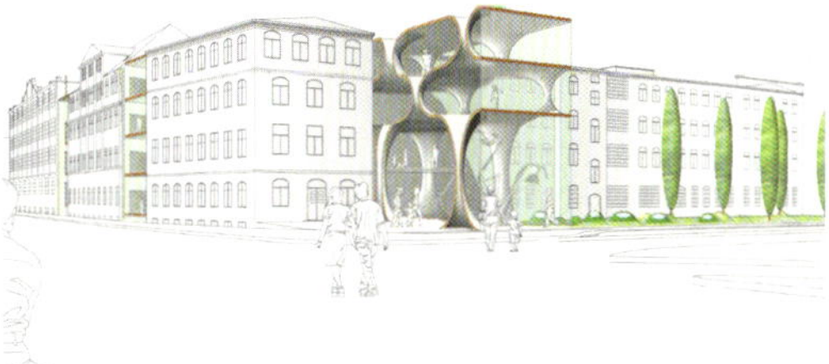

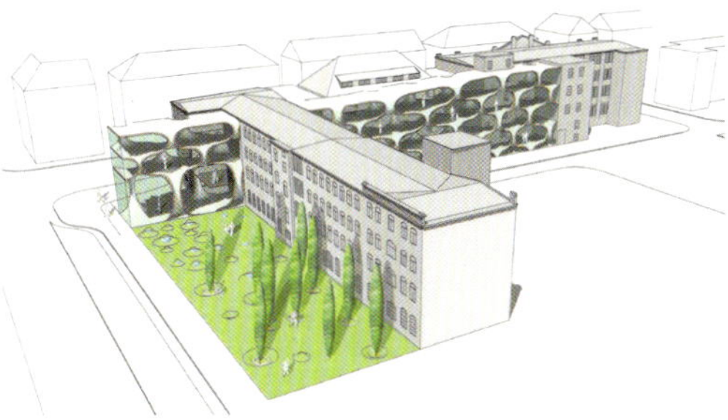

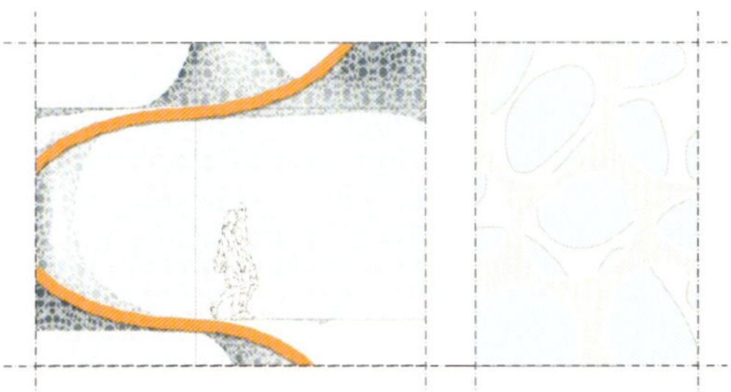

# HOUSE OF THE FUTURE

13-07-2007

**IMAGINED BY** Behnisch Architects in cooperation with M. Bilow and U. Knaack
**KEYWORDS** structure, façade, modules, functions, adaptability
**PERFORMANCE** adaptability

This building was developed for the campus of IIT in Chicago with the purpose of highlighting new and future technologies. To counteract the problem that, upon completion, the building would no longer be a house of the future, the façade was developed as a load-bearing frame that can accommodate changing new and innovative components. In a first version, functional components have been arranged across the entire façade depending on the requirements of the interior space and the geographic orientation. In this example, functional panels for solar power and collector surfaces, for example, are mounted on the southern part of the façade; while the northern façade is equipped with highly insulated or translucent elements.

filling materials

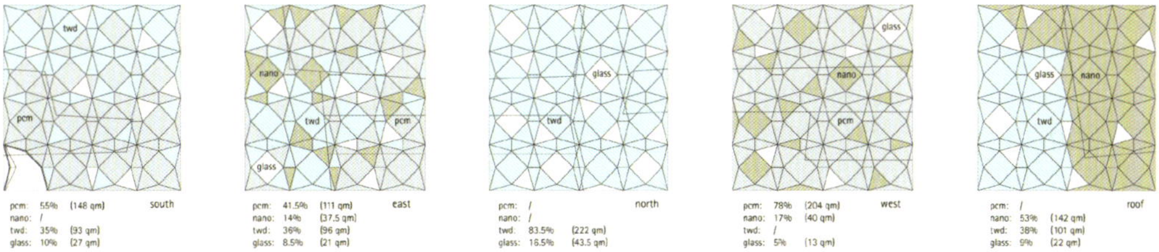


special interior cladding
including capillar mats for heating and cooling

overlay

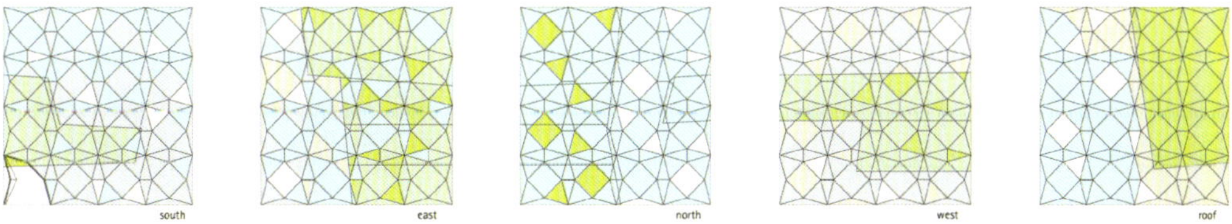


possible locations for pv-panels and solar collectors (220 qm)

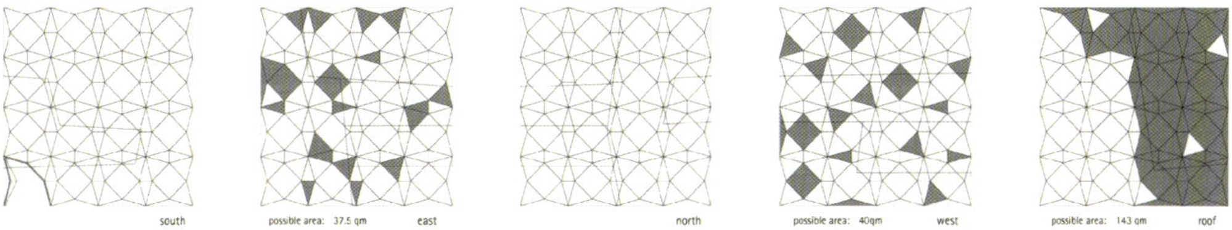


alternative
pv-foils (duennfilm-technologie in "siebdruckmuster")

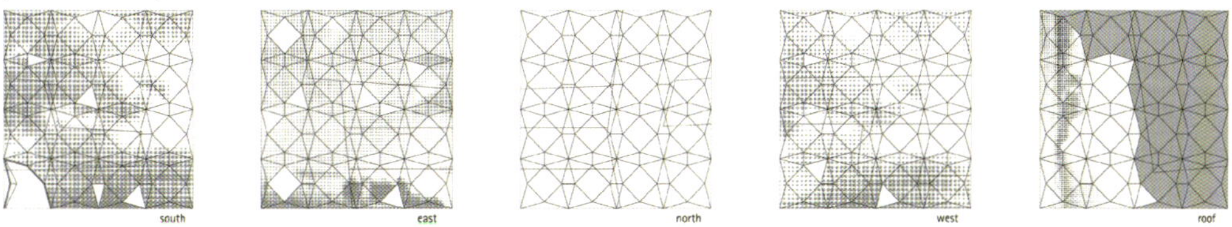


powerhaus facade schemes
behnisch architects
july 16, 2007

# IKEA 2.0

30-11-2009

**IMAGINED BY** Holger Strauss
**KEYWORDS** layered construction, modular, system, lighting, ventilation, insulation, sun shading, transparency, low cost, façade, plastics
**PERFORMANCE** upgradeability

This façade is based on an upgradeable system, adaptable to the funds of the respective user. It can be started with the cheap and lightweight base model, and extended at a later stage by buying additional parts.
The base model offers the basic façade prerequisites only – protection against weather influences. Functions such as shading devices and ventilation systems can be added from the "component catalogue" if and when required.

# INTERACTIVE LIGHT SCULPTURE

21-02-2011

**IMAGINED BY** Leland Curtis, guided by U. Knaack, T. Klein and M. Bilow
Part of the Future Envelope class at Penn State University
**KEYWORDS** structure, glass, light, moving, transparency
**PERFORMANCE** interactivity

The façade attempts to absorb the unique story of each visitor and reflects it, combined with the impressions left by all who have recently interacted with it.
This is accomplished through an interactive sculpture installed in the storefront windows. It lights up as people pass and records their motion to be replayed later. The result is a smoothly flowing light sculpture that embodies the movement of the city. The sculpture is located at pedestrian level where it can be most interactive.

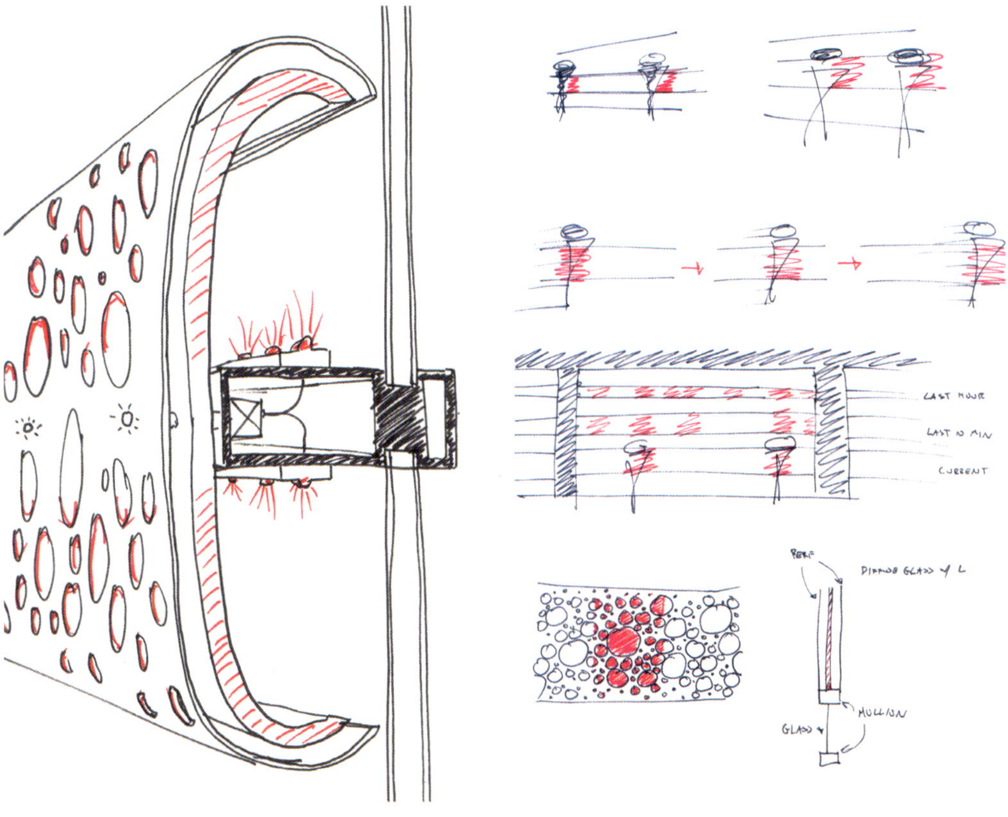

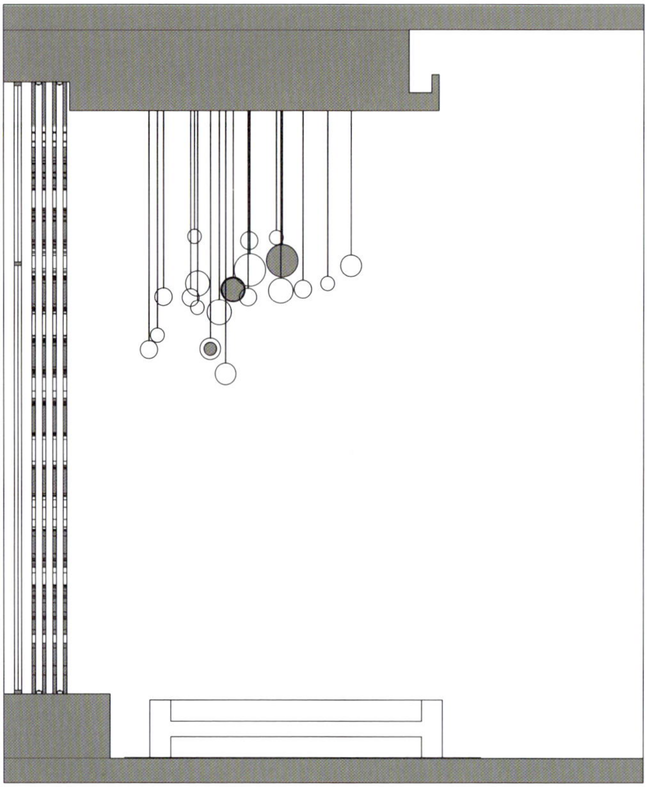

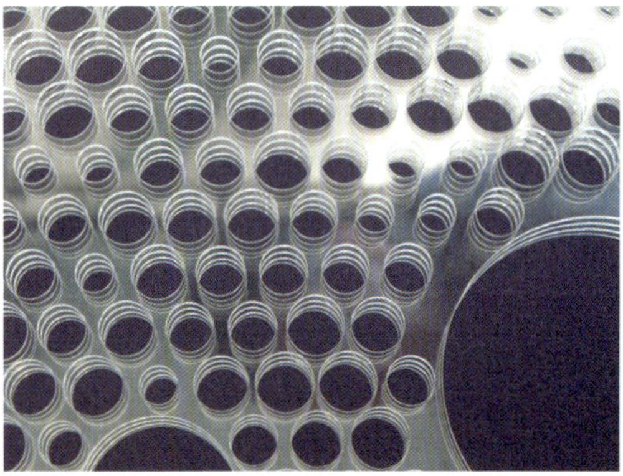

# REVOLVER STATION

15-08-2003

**IMAGINED BY** Marcel Bilow
**KEYWORDS** structure, movement, free-form space
**PERFORMANCE** moving

Throughout the ages, railway stations have been locations of technology manifestation. Old stations still radiate the upswing of industrialization, and are popular tourist attractions. As crossing points for many railway lines and other public transportation, modern railway stations are key locations and often the centre of a city.
But what if new railway lines such as high-speed lines need to be added? This concept exploits the principle of a revolver: similar to the rounds in a chamber, the trains rotate in a giant revolver. Travellers can board and de-board when the train has reached a certain position within the revolver, just as the train can leave the station when it has reached the desired track position. This concept requires less space and manifests new technologies in a breathtaking facility that turns travel into a new adventure.

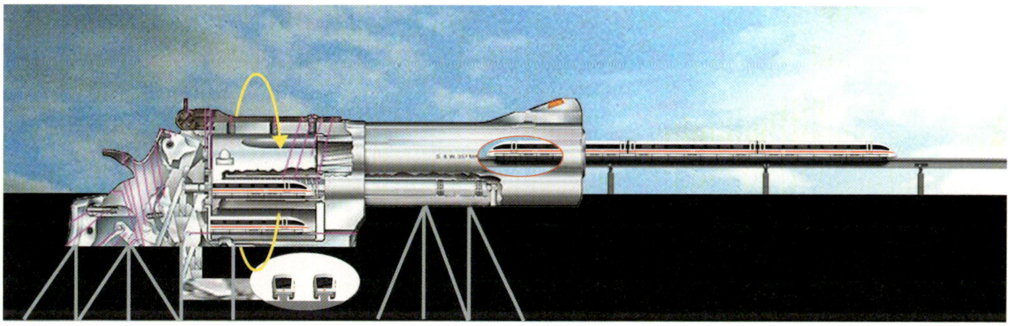

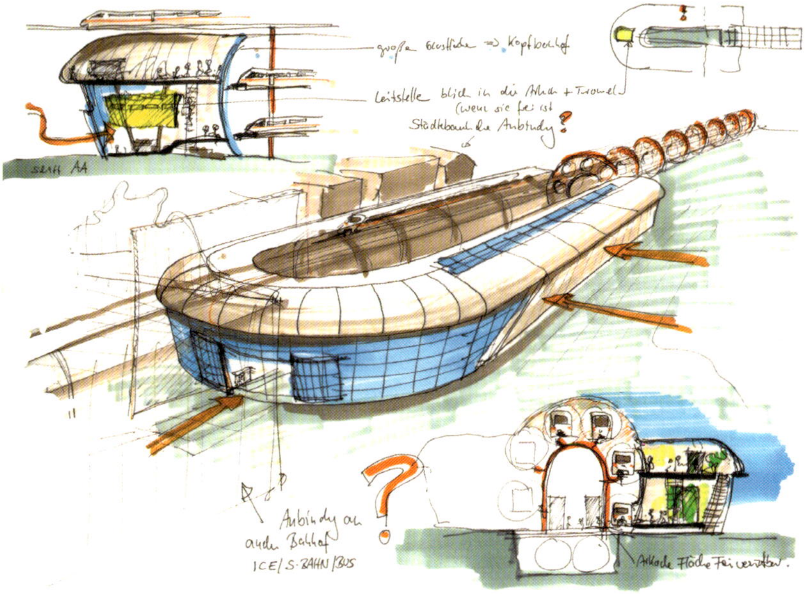

# SELF-TIDYING FLOOR

28-04-2009

**IMAGINED BY** Thiemo Ebbert
**KEYWORDS** self-organizing, floor, dynamic material, interior, exterior
**PERFORMANCE** easy to clean

A commonly known problem: children's bedrooms or public squares after major events have one thing in common. It is a lot of work to tidy up the mess. The self-tidying floor is made of an adaptable material, which can rise and lower in programmed patterns. The waves thus created transport everything on the floor to one spot, where it can easily be removed.

Additionally, the floor-coating can be stabilized in defined shapes. Thus, dynamic landscapes can be created to be used for public events, skate parks, etc.

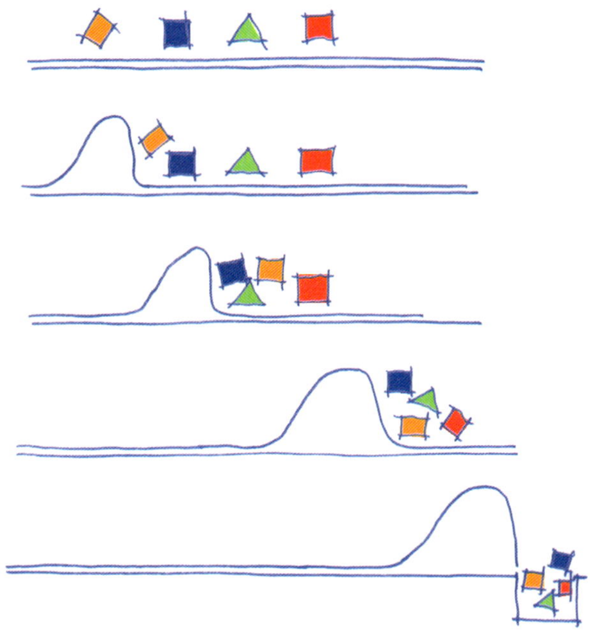

# URBAN SPACE ENVELOPE

25-09-2007

**IMAGINED BY** Behnisch Architects in cooperation with imagine structures and imagine envelope
**KEYWORDS** umbrella, structure, climate, sustainability, comfort
**PERFORMANCE** space coverage

This roof concept was developed for a competition in Rome. The goal was to create a comfortable outside space with the use of individual umbrellas. Each of the umbrellas fulfills a different function within the urban environment; in their entirety they create sustainable and comfortable shelter. In addition to classic functions such as sun protection, the umbrellas can serve to collect rain water or generate electricity by means of photovoltaic cells. Light mist can be sprayed from the umbrella shafts to cool the entire plaza by adiabatic cooling. The use of solar power and collected rain water makes this concept virtually energy self-sufficient.

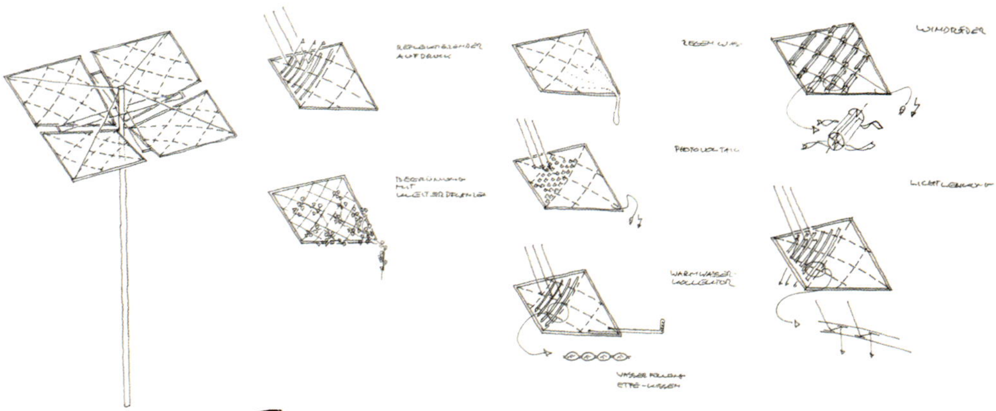

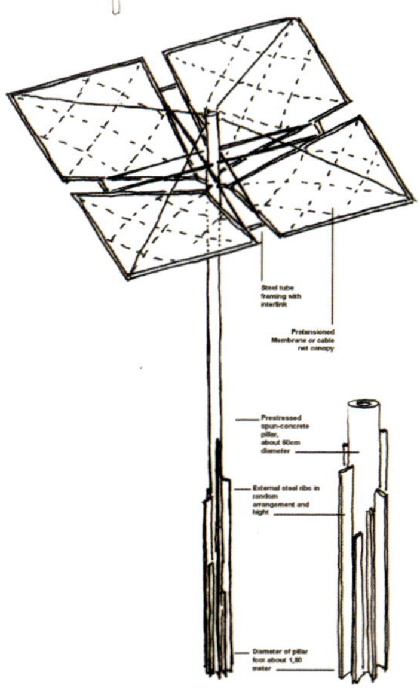


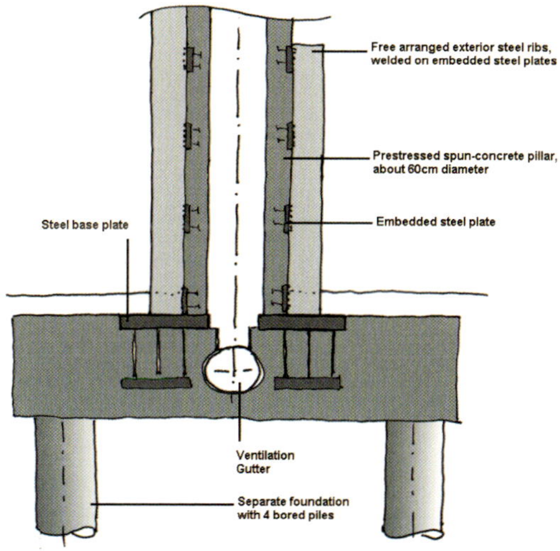

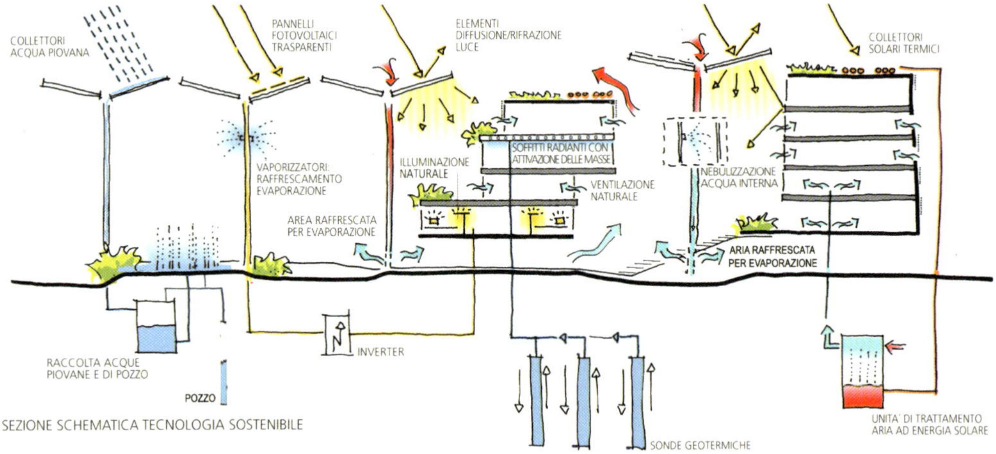

SEZIONE SCHEMATICA TECNOLOGIA SOSTENIBILE

# 4.2. COMFORT

Comfort defines the technical quality of a building / building component in terms of air (air exchange, air quality, draught, etc.), radiation (incident solar radiation, diffuse radiation and shading, etc.), noise (noise level, noise distribution, etc.), temperature (inside and outside temperatures, changes in temperature, etc.) as well as humidity (water, rain, air humidity, etc.).

# BLOOM SOLAR SHADING

05-02-2011

**IMAGINED BY** Mahzad Tashakori, guided by U. Knaack, T. Klein and M. Bilow
Part of the Future Envelope class at Penn State University
**KEYWORDS** dynamic, shading, pattern, bio inspired, façade
**PERFORMANCE** shading

The idea is to create solar shading modules that form a second façade layer for buildings in arid climates such as Iran. This system can be mounted on existing mullions of glazing or be built as a twin layered façade.
Solar panels are opened and closed manually from the inside, based on the amount of shading desired. Ropes pull the panels out. In the model, they are also actuated by SMA wires, which means that the system can be run by heat sensors or computers. To enhance the performance, PV cells could be used as panels themselves to store energy. With thermal sensors they could be integrated in a building management system to control the blooming based on the solar angle at different times and in different climates. Stored solar energy could run the motor that opens up the panels. Arduino in the form of an environmental sensor can be effectively used in this system to capture the environmental data and affect the computational model of the façade in the building management system and thus operate the modules.

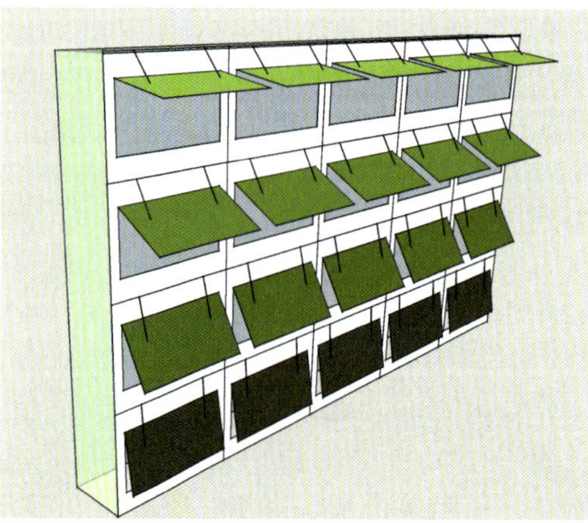

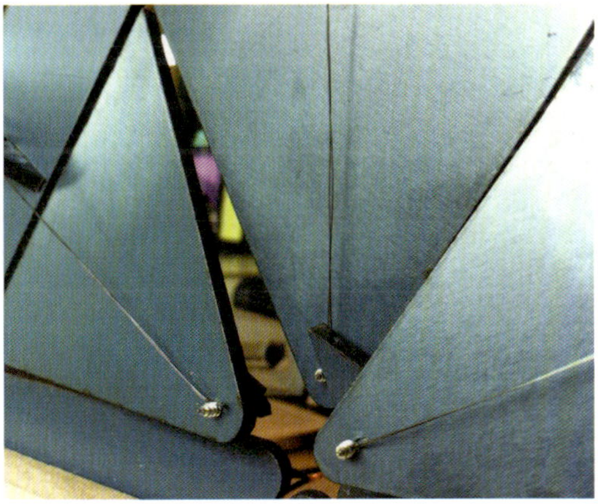

# BREATHING CONCRETE

12-05-2005

**IMAGINED BY** Marcel Bilow
**KEYWORDS** concrete, façade cladding, ventilation, breathing
**PERFORMANCE** air ventilation

Beside the necessary reinforcement of a concrete wall, a fine mesh of ventilation pores could be integrated into the concrete that allows wind to flow through a massive wall element.
In a first test, a set of small breathing valves was produced with rapid prototyping to create an ultra fine 3-dimensional structure that allows air flow but keeps the water out during rainy conditions.

The goal of this concept is a type of reinforcement that provides strength as well as the possibility to integrate air valves.

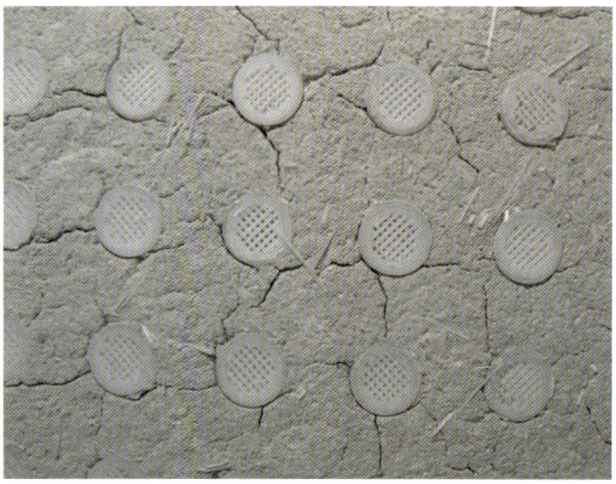
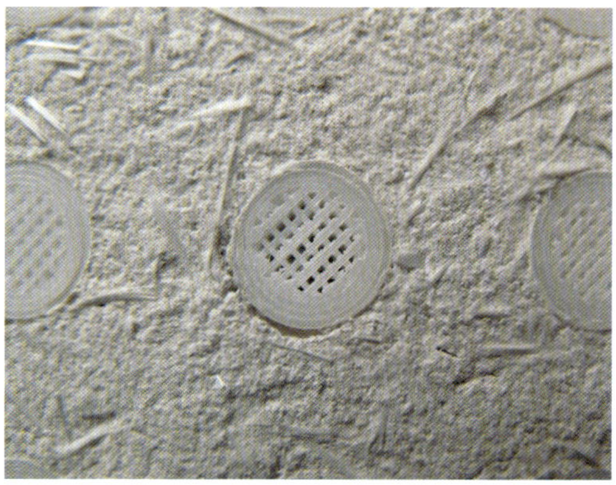

# FOAM SCREEN
13-03-2009

IMAGINED BY imagine Klappergassenworkshop
KEYWORDS foam, structure, building material, analysis, 3D Printing
PERFORMANCE shading

This idea to add a layer of foam to the window or façade element evolved from searching for ways to direct incident light. By using thinner or thicker layers, foam can transmit more or less light. At a close distance, the façade appears almost transparent; with greater distance the visible number of bubbles in the foam increases, thereby decreasing the transparency. The façade appears translucent. Energy input decreases at the same rate as the transparency is reduced.

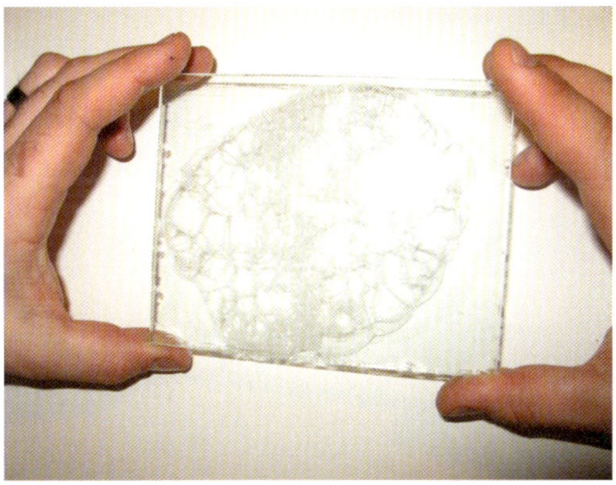

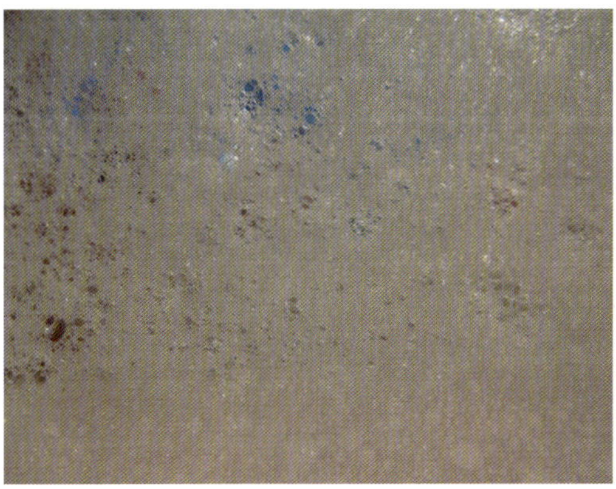
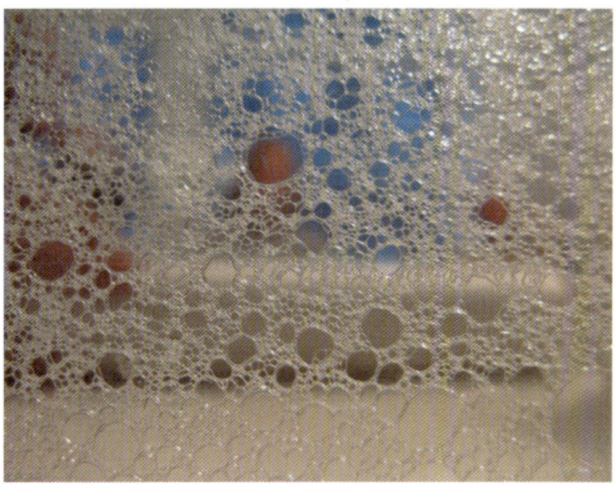

# LIQUID FAÇADE

25-19-2009

**IMAGINED BY** Francesco Goia
**KEYWORDS** water storage, façade, energy storage, system
**PERFORMANCE** energy storage

The idea of a liquid façade is not new; water inside a façade layer absorbs solar energy, thus reducing the temperature of the indoor space.
This principle can be further developed by adding a second water-bearing façade layer. In the outer layer, water cools the façade. The thermal energy gain can be used on the inside to heat the room. Depending on the season and current weather conditions, the two streams of water can be regulated to create an optimum indoor climate throughout the year.

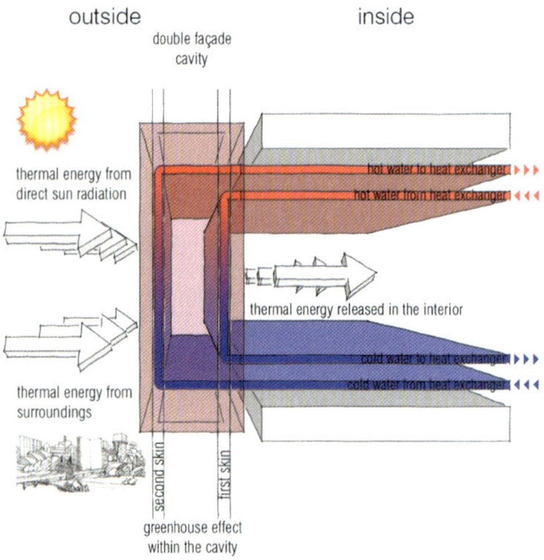


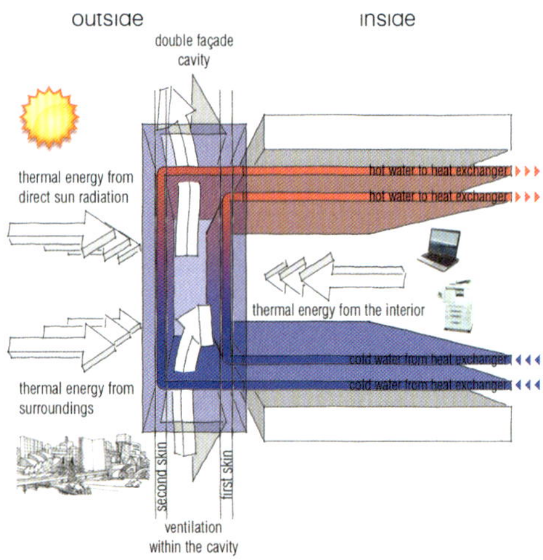


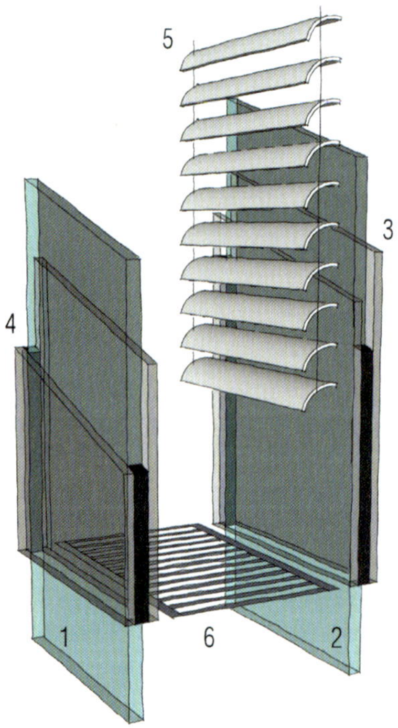


*6.9_ Double duo-liquids façade: diagrammatic sketch of façade' layers.*

1_outer liquid layer
2_inner double glass panel
3_double glass panel with gap for inner liquid layer
4_double glass panel with gap for outer liquid layer
5_sunshade device
6_double skin cavity for ventilation

# MICRO-SHINGLES
30-11-2009

IMAGINED BY Lisa Rammig
KEYWORDS self-organizing, ventilation, moving, self-cleaning, interactive, adapting, envelope, building physics
PERFORMANCE weather adaptability

This micro structure has the ability to adapt to current weather conditions. During dry and sunny conditions, it is open and air can ventilate through. If it comes in contact with humidity, e.g. rain, the structure closes and forms a water-tight layer, which opens again when dried by the sun. In its open state, the structure is ventilated again and residual humidity is dried off. Since the structure is closed during rain periods, the cumulated dirt is washed off and the structure is cleaned.

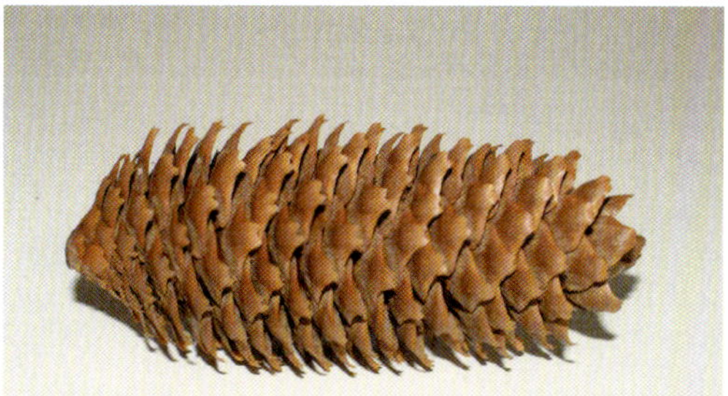

# MIRRORING PV-CELLS

01-05-2009

**IMAGINED BY** Thiemo Ebbert
**KEYWORDS** system, energy generating, PV, light-transporting, sun-shading, façade, glass, 0 - 10 years
**PERFORMANCE** sun shading & creating energy

Highly reflective solar cells are mounted perpendicular to the façade. The cells provide several advantages: Sun-shading for the window below, a light shelf function to reflect additional daylight into the room, and generation of electricity. So far the system is well known.

Innovative Thin-Film PV cells provide a very high grade of reflexion comparable to a mirror. Thus the light-shelf effect is improved. And, the more light is reflected, the less is absorbed in the cell. The cell itself does not heat up as much as a conventional one. Hence it provides a higher efficiency.

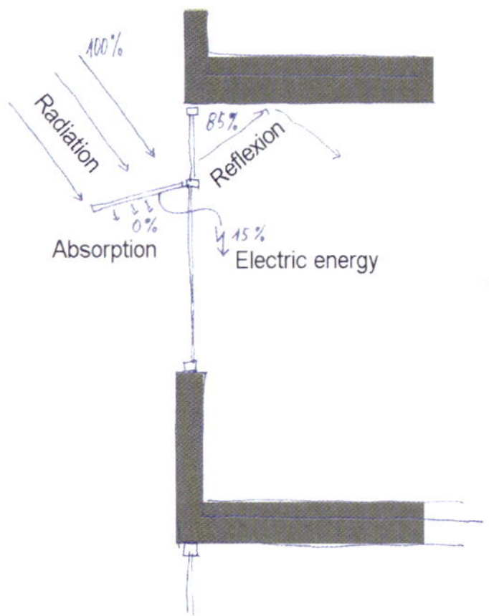


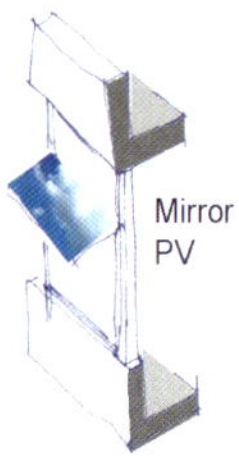


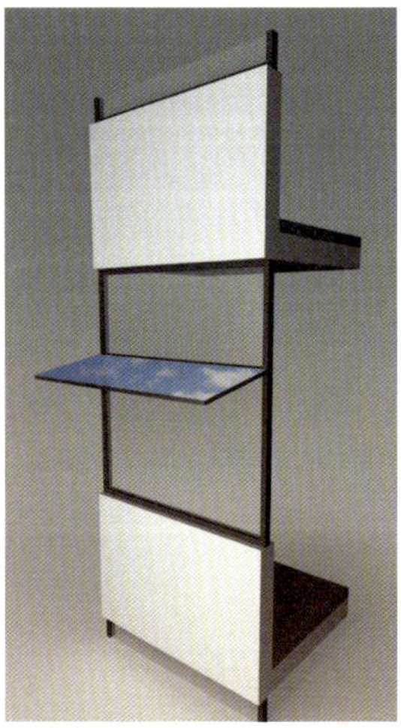

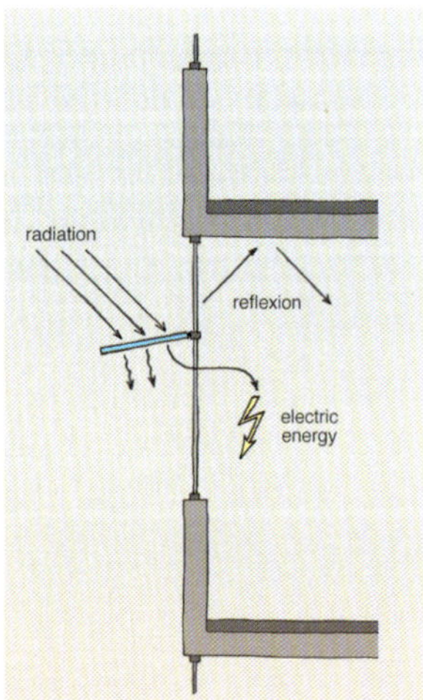

# POCKET FAÇADE

05-04-2011

**IMAGINED BY** Michael Costa supported by U. Knaack, T. Klein and M. Bilow
Part of the Future Envelope class at Penn State University
**KEYWORDS** air, adapting, façade, system, foil
**PERFORMANCE** insulation

The idea is based on using air as an insulation agent by creating an air pocket within the wall cavity. Essentially, this means combining traditional elements of building construction, and layering them into one system that acts as a breathable skin. In order to protect and save historic materials, for example, the surrounding space needs to exhibit consistent temperatures. A major variable would be the climate change throughout the day and year, which requires a movable element to control solar glare.

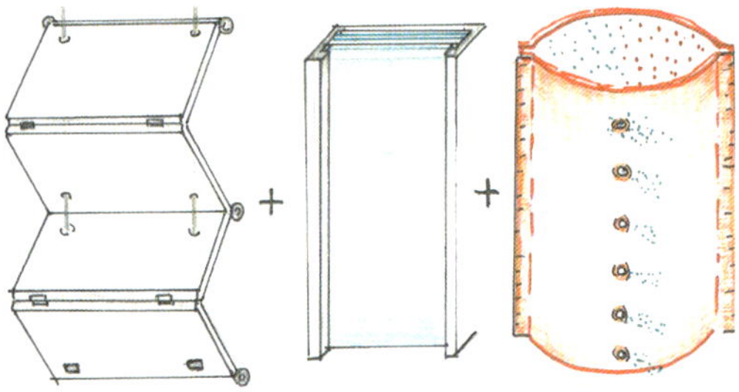

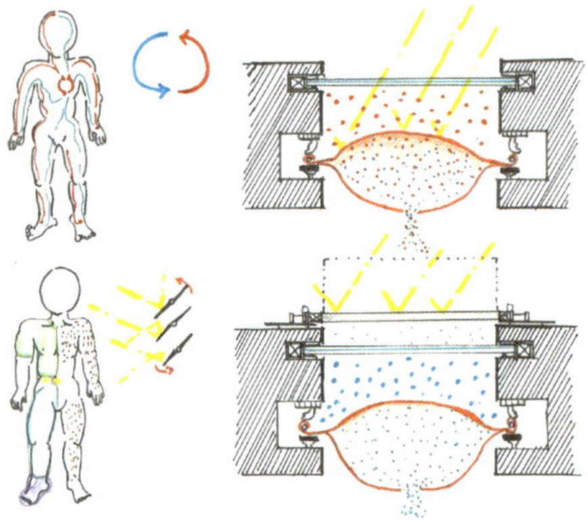

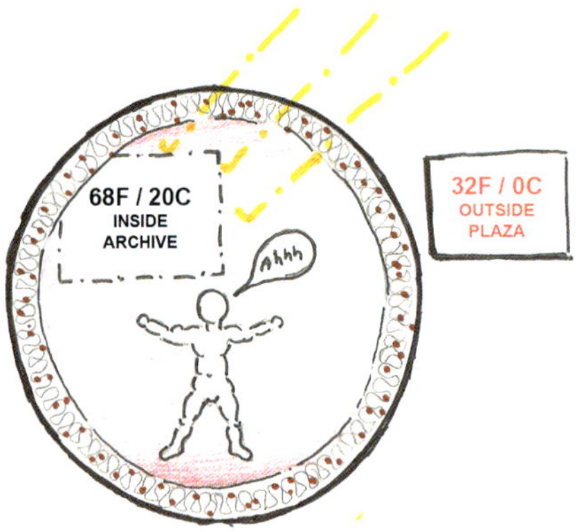
68F / 20C
INSIDE
ARCHIVE
Ahhh
32F / 0C
OUTSIDE
PLAZA

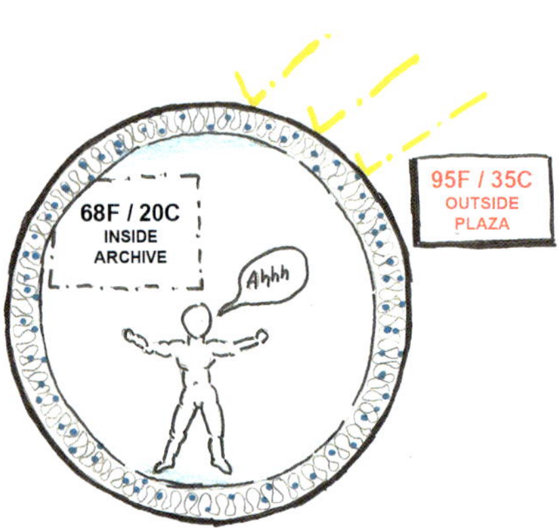
68F / 20C
INSIDE
ARCHIVE
Ahhh
95F / 35C
OUTSIDE
PLAZA

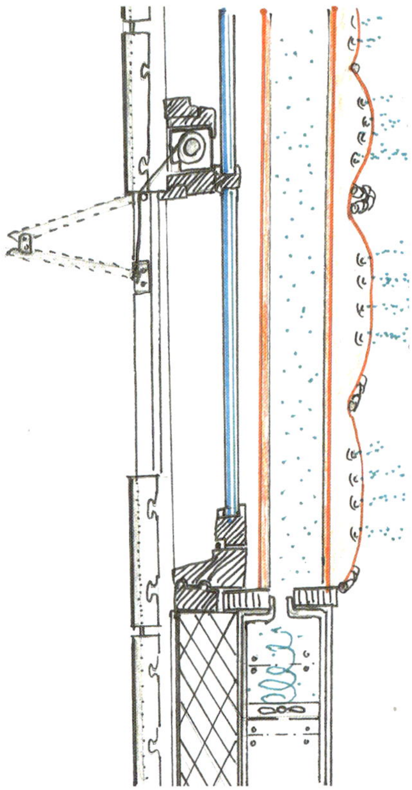

# SMART HOUSE

05-07-2010

IMAGINED BY Behnisch Architects in cooperation with Transsolar and imagine envelope
KEYWORDS sun shading, adaptability, window, façade
PERFORMANCE shading

In order to realize the best possible shading for the building, the design for this sun shading system is based on the working method of an eye lid. Studying the sun angle determined optimum angles for the curved panels depending on their geographic orientation to provide optimum daylight yield while ensuring the best possible shading. Thus, the façade offers transparency with efficient sun protection. The size of the elements is scalable, and they can be customized for any purpose and for different types of construction.

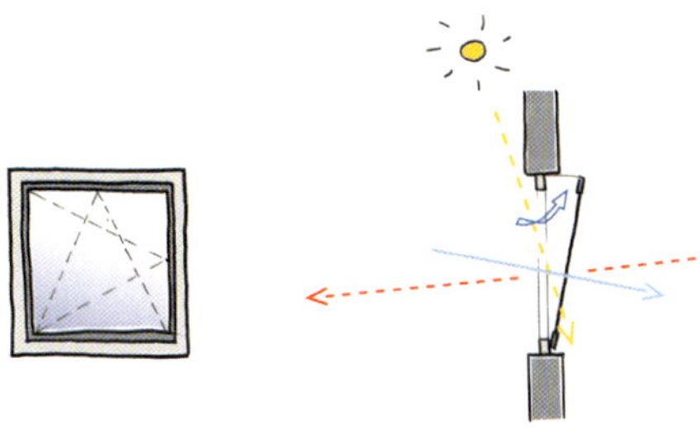

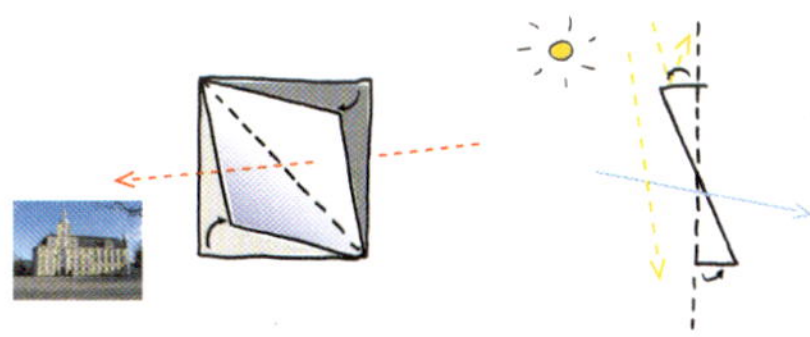

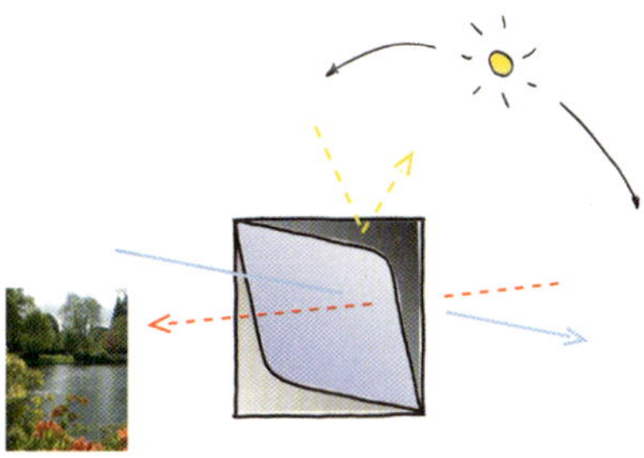

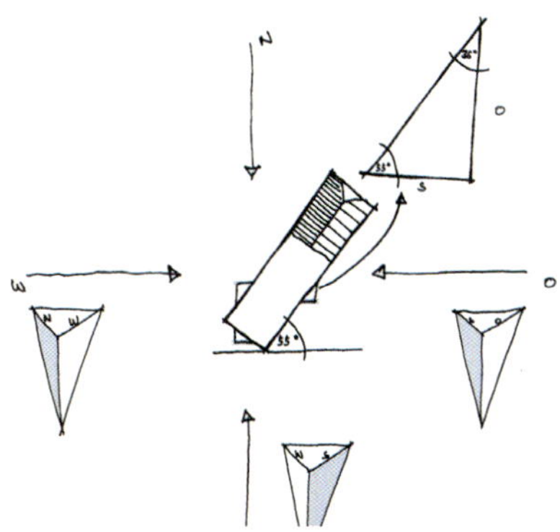

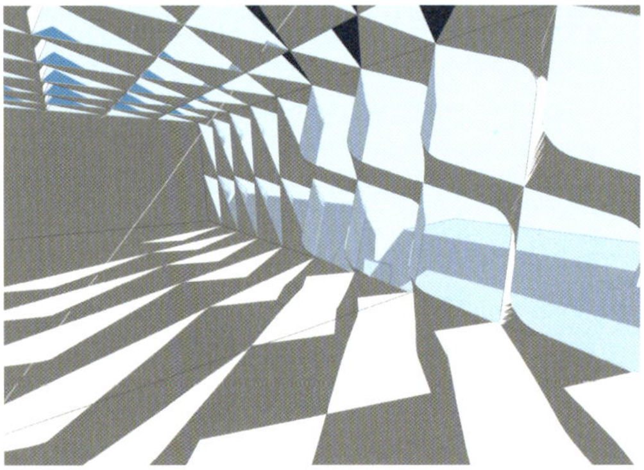

# SUN SCREEN CHAMBERS
30-11-2009

IMAGINED BY Christian Wedi
KEYWORDS layered construction, modular, interactive, sun shading, control, heating/cooling, liquid, adaptability, façade, glass, water, unknown material
PERFORMANCE shading

Transparency is an important factor for the atmosphere and comfort in a room, because daylight influences the complacency of human beings. But heat loss through these transparent parts of the façade is a fundamental problem, which also leads to a sense of discomfort. When the sun shines on this façade, the energy is stored and the windows change to an opaque state. The more intense the incident sunlight, the hotter the temperature in the cavity, and the more opaque the windows become. Solar energy is used to prevent the building from overheating and to provide glare protection for the user.

# 4.3. SECURITY

This topic covers the load-bearing function of a building part including sub items such as own weight, live load, wind load and extraordinary loads. Fire, intentional damage and protection against burglary are included as well.

BOMB BLASTING STRUCTURE
BOMB BLASTING FAÇADE
FIRE-PROTECTIVE FOG
FIRE-PROTECTIVE SHUTTER
INFLATABLE DIVIDING WALL
PROTECTIVE SECOND SKIN
SHAPE MEMORY ENVELOPE
WATER BALLOONS

# BOMB BLASTING STRUCTURE

02-07-2011

**IMAGINED BY** Holger Techen
**KEYWORDS** blast mitigation, security
**PERFORMANCE** system ductility

Based on the idea of the bomb blasting façade, the overall façade structure could be ductile. Not single façade elements or windows feature predetermined breaking points to reduce the impact of an explosion, but the entire substructure of the façade is spring-mounted. The resulting elasticity must be adjusted such that wind force alone does not activate the springs. The combination of material and construction is essential to produce options for a yielding building envelope.

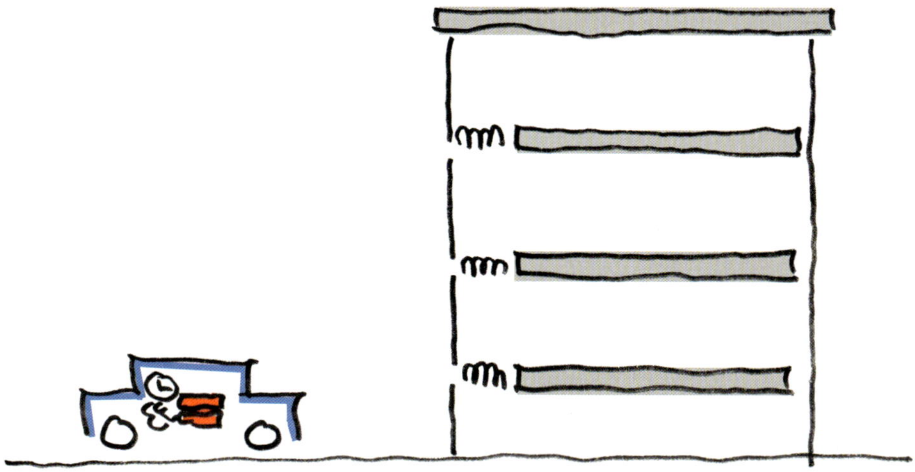

# BOMB BLASTING FAÇADE

02-07-2011

**IMAGINED BY** Holger Techen
**KEYWORDS** blast mitigation, security
**PERFORMANCE** system ductility

Protection against terror attacks is a central criterion when designing government buildings or buildings for electric power companies and financial institutions. In addition to access control, strengthening the building envelope provides efficient protection. The façade can be reinforced in two ways. Limiting the window size, strengthening the frame and increasing glass thickness can all aid in fortifying a façade against explosion pressure. However, the true effectiveness of such measures remains uncertain because stress through explosion is hard to predict and define. As an alternative to fortification, the pressure waves from an explosion and the resulting damages can be significantly reduced by opening the façade. Predetermined breaking points allow façade elements or windows to swing open, eliminating the risk of breaking glass and shards flying through the air.

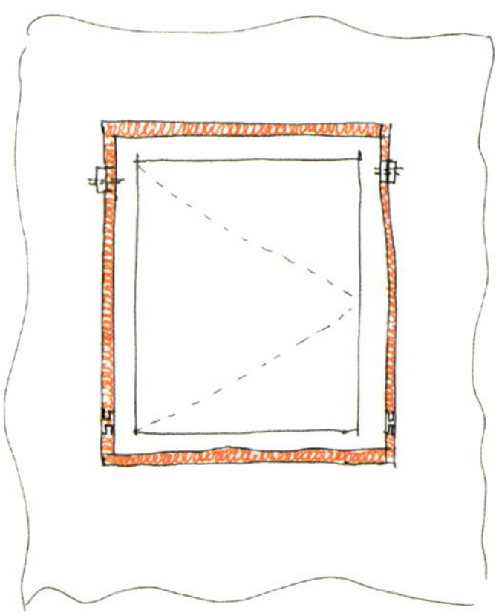

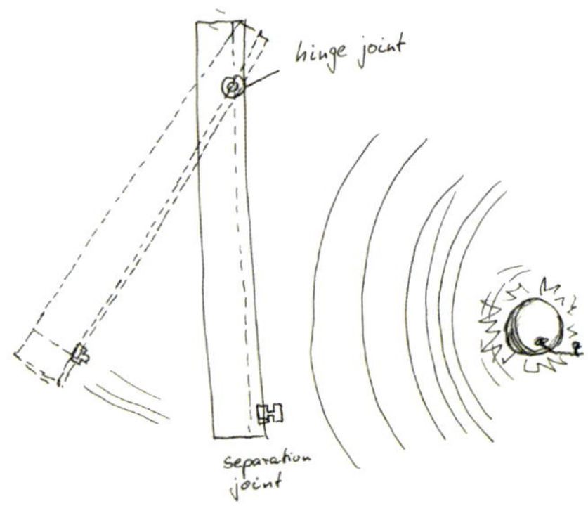

# FIRE-PROTECTIVE FOG

24-04-2008

IMAGINED BY T. Klein, U. Knaack, M. Bilow
KEYWORDS fire, protection, system, mechanical system
PERFORMANCE fire safety

A concept used in shipbuilding has been adapted in order to build glass doors without fire-protective glazing. Fireboats at sea spray atomized water at a short distance around the fireboat to reduce the high temperatures radiating from a close-by burning ship. This self-protecting function can be applied to fire-protection doors in architecture. The goal is to cool surfaces with minimum amounts of water.

# FIRE-PROTECTIVE SHUTTER

24-04-2008

IMAGINED BY T. Klein, U. Knaack, M. Bilow
KEYWORDS fire, protection, system, mechanical system
PERFORMANCE fire safety

Fireproof doors must feature special fire-protective glazing if they are to be transparent. To save the cost for special glazing, this concept adds an extra layer to provide adequate fire protection. On that side of the door where the fire occurs, interlocking fireproof slats drop from the ceiling to ensure fire protection.

# INFLATABLE DIVIDING WALL

07-09-2009

**IMAGINED BY** Thiemo Ebbert
**KEYWORDS** temporary structure, refurbishment
**PERFORMANCE** separating

Most of the older office buildings no longer comply with current energy standards. If such buildings are refurbished, the existing curtain wall façade is usually replaced. This means that the entire building has to be vacated, and all employees have to be relocated for the duration of the construction. This process usually takes a lot of time and causes expenses for interim-locations and the relocation itself.

The inflatable wall makes it possible to renew a curtain wall while the building is in operation. It is composed of inflatable cushions which span from floor to ceiling. Fully inflated, these cushions shield the room against dirt and provide thermal insulation during the construction phase. Transparent parts in the temporary wall ensure that sufficient daylight penetrates the room.

By separating the construction zone from the actual office area, the façade, the building services (located along the façade) and all necessary connections to interior walls can be refurbished more quickly and economically. Construction time is minimized and there is no need to relocate the staff.

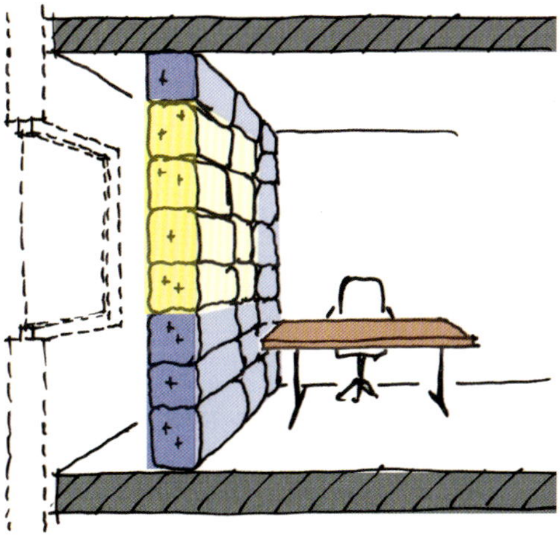

# PROTECTIVE SECOND SKIN

30-11-2009

**IMAGINED BY** Holger Strauss
**KEYWORDS** layered construction, composite, security, easy to recycle, façade, paper
**PERFORMANCE** bomb blasting resistance

This suspended construction made of paint and paper forms a second skin providing protection against the detonation of a bomb.
The energy occurring during an explosion is absorbed by the material of the second skin, and when it is destroyed, it can be recycled easily.

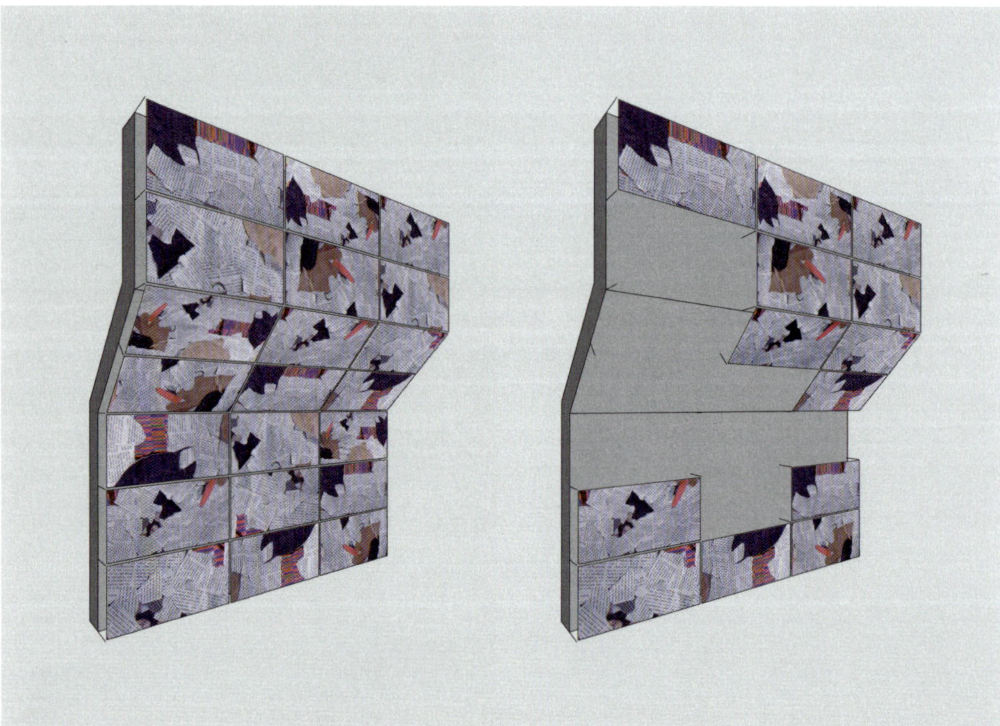

# SHAPE MEMORY ENVELOPE
15-07-2008

**IMAGINED BY** U. Knaack
**KEYWORDS** crash protection, system, mechanical system
**PERFORMANCE** crash protection

Shape memory alloys can return to their original shape after deformation. If an alloy is deformed in its cold state, it will return to its original shape by heating it above the transition temperature. If such a material is used for façade cladding, it can, after deformation, be returned to its original state by the sun and the ambient temperature. If, for example, a car runs into a façade, the façade can thus heal itself.

# WATER BALLOONS

30-11-2009

**IMAGINED BY** Catrin Höferlin
**KEYWORDS** security, control, liquid, interior, foil, water, façade
**PERFORMANCE** fire protection

This unusual fire resistant wall is made of water balloons, which, in the case of fire, provides safety by preventing the fire from spreading. This device is very simple but can serve as an artistic expression or piece of art in addition to its protective function.

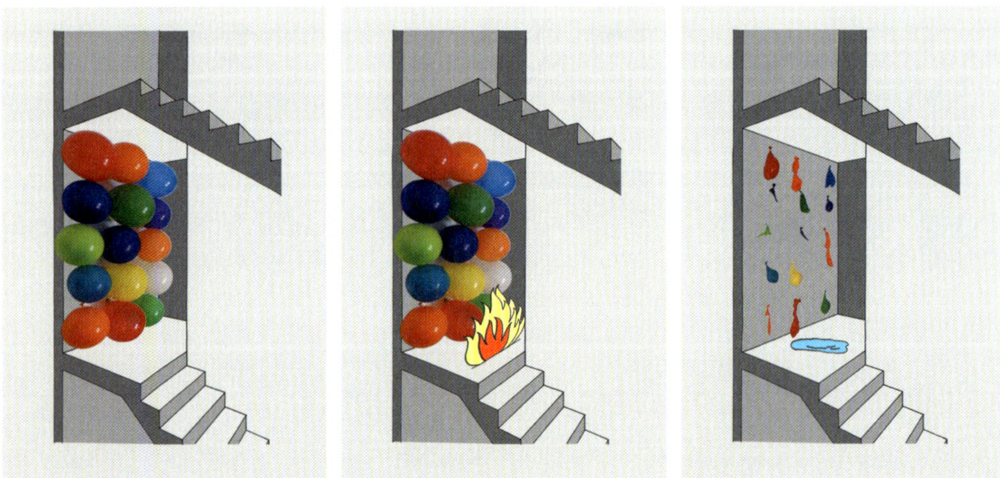

# 4.4. SUSTAINABILITY

The subject area of sustainability deals with the global topic energy; energy gain, protection from energy loss and/or incident energy, and embedded energy, i.e. energy needed for the production of materials and constructions. But questions as to the durability of a construction and the possibility of maintaining it permanently and possible recycling after its useful life has ended are all aspects covered under this topic.

# CAR TIRES

30-11-2009

**IMAGINED BY** Daniel Arztmann
**KEYWORDS** pneumatic, insulation, sun shading, transparency, low cost, façade, foil, plastics, membrane, waste
**PERFORMANCE** recycling

Used car tires produce huge amounts of waste that takes up large areas of storage space. However, this waste can be used to create a façade. To obtain water tightness and to regulate the climate, shopping bags are used as membranes around the tires. By using different bags with various properties, the condition and atmosphere in the interior space can be controlled, and transparent parts are separated from opaque parts.

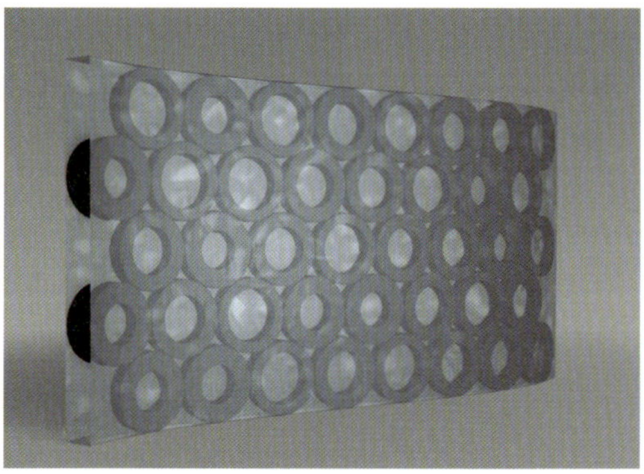

# MULTI-LAYERED GLASS

15-07-2011

IMAGINED BY U. Knaack
KEYWORDS glass, layers, insulation, recycling, separation
PERFORMANCE recycling

In architecture, the classic glass plane evolved from a single pane to a double pane, and now to a triple pane. Insulation values are optimized, and coatings on the glass can further improve its performance. But what will be next? Window glass can no longer be recycled; it is being down-cycled, meaning it is turned into drinking bottles, because we can no longer dissect the different materials that are included in the glass.

Can we expect multi-layered glass consisting of 5 and more panes? If so, we should make sure it is uncoated – consisting only of pure float glass that can easily be recycled.

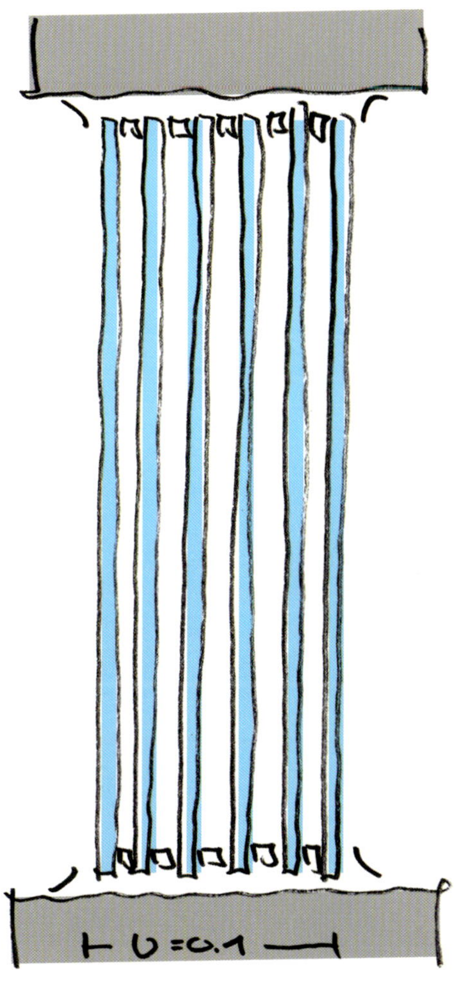

# PLASTIC PROPERTIES I
07-04-2011

**IMAGINED BY** Richard Kelly, guided by U. Knaack, T. Klein and M. Bilow
Part of the Future Envelope class at Penn State University
**KEYWORDS** manipulating plastic, recycling, façade, system
**PERFORMANCE** recycling

The idea is to develop a cheap and easy process that stimulates the creativity of the producer. By manipulating the properties of plastic bags, a highly accessible material, anyone can form, shape and produce specific designs based on the single modular unit of a plastic bag. Meant as a temporary spatial solution, these skins have a short shelf life, enabling a continuation in creativity and adaptation for the occupant.

Composed of thin plastic, the translucent material is a good buffer against light, sound, and air; creating a simple shield between a conditioned and an unconditioned space. Options include manipulating the plastic into air pockets, water collectors, soil containers for a green wall, for example, sound absorption/reflectors etc.

The main idea is to add utilitarian functions to simple, temporary and habitable spaces, so that the user becomes a creator; by altering, manipulating and transforming his/her space depending on a particular use, condition and/or time. This one material can be easily manipulated to conform to a multiple of constraints and options.

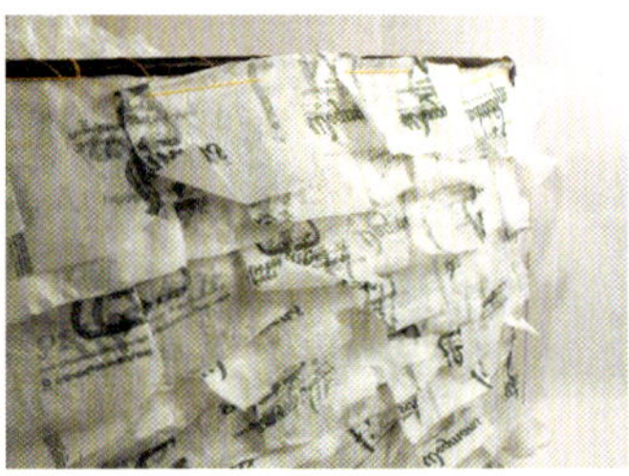

# PLASTIC PROPERTIES II

07-04-2011

**IMAGINED BY** Richard Kelly, guided by U. Knaack, T. Klein and M. Bilow
Part of the Future Envelope class at Penn State University
**KEYWORDS** manipulating plastic, recycling, façade, system
**PERFORMANCE** recycling

The idea is to find an easy method to create a façade skin that can be erected within a short period of time, on a low budget, and that provides maximum use and habitation. The principle demonstrates the capability of plastic as a diffuser of ambient light; creating visual interest with different colors and textures resulting from the variations of plastic used to form the skin. While the plastic serves as a light diffuser, it also forms an insulating layer for the occupant. It allows air to ventilate through the façade, while still providing protection from the thermal properties of the exterior space.

The main idea is to utilize and manipulate simple materials to create visually and thermally comfortable spaces.

# WASTE BOTTLE FAÇADE

02-05-2011

**IMAGINED BY** Zachary Jones supported by U. Knaack, T. Klein and M. Bilow
Part of the Future Envelope class at Penn State University
**KEYWORDS** façade, recycling, waste material, light, building material
**PERFORMANCE** recycling

An 'active' passive system. This concept uses a panel system that sustains a passive cooling system. Based on existing solar refrigerator systems, the units could be expanded into a wall system for areas with high year round temperatures. The system could be used to assist in the rebuilding of Haiti or similar areas of destruction. It utilizes rubble as the outer layer. This layer heats up and evaporates the moisture into the dirt, which would consequently draw out heat from the interior space.

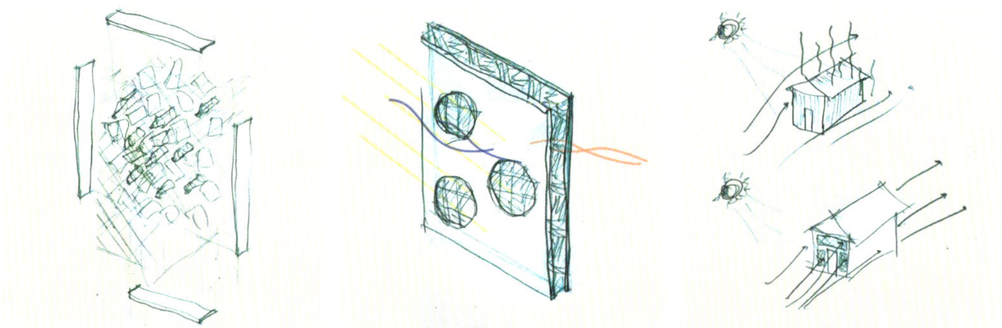

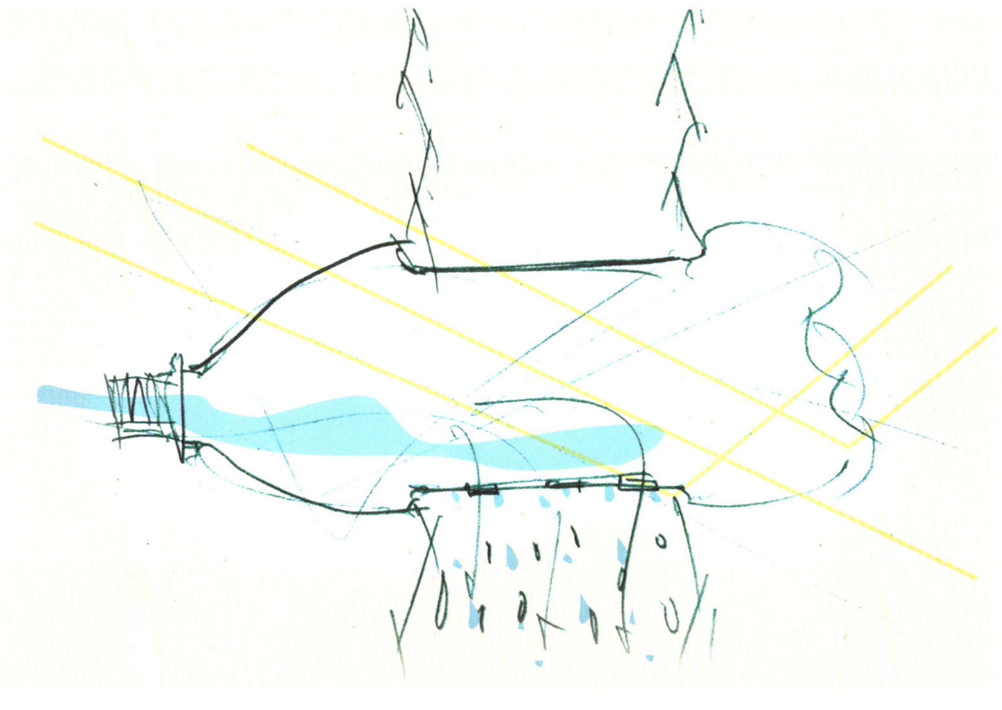

# 4.5. MATERIAL

The section about the performance of materials includes material winning, and the manufacturing as well as installation of a construction on site. Material properties and their durability are discussed here. Examples are given for various new materials as well as possible new methods of "winning" materials (production, material properties and assembly).

# BMW HOUR GLASS

05-04-2008

**IMAGINED BY** Matthias Michel, Holger Techen
**KEYWORDS** transforming material, BMW hour glass
**PERFORMANCE** invisible/transparent structure

The essential performance (transparency) of the material (polycarbonate) is exploited and combined with the material's load-bearing capacity and high processability. This broadens the range of possible applications significantly. However, it also requires new solutions in joining technology and new consideration in terms of approval specifications for above surface construction.

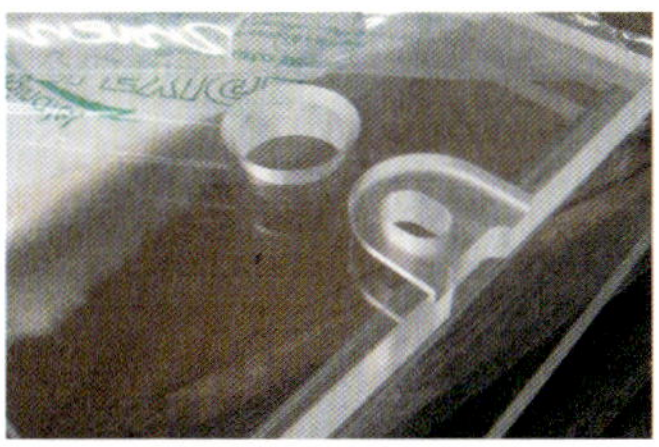

# CABLE-CAR CARACAS

29-07-2007

**IMAGINED BY** M. Bilow for Urban Think Tank
**KEYWORDS** construction, structure, fiber reinforced concrete
**PERFORMANCE** production

A production method for the cable-car project in Caracas planned by Urban Think Tank to allow for a light roof construction for a new cable-car station.
The goal of the project was to develop a production method that would allow the inhabitants of the favelas in the area to participate in building the cable-car station to create jobs.

The concept uses a sandwich construction formed by multiple layers comprising a metallic base layer, a core insulation and fiber reinforced concrete. Injecting fiber concrete into deeper impressions in the mold makes for a rigid ribbed structure after curing.

The roof elements are prefabricated on site and then lifted onto the load-bearing frame by helicopter.

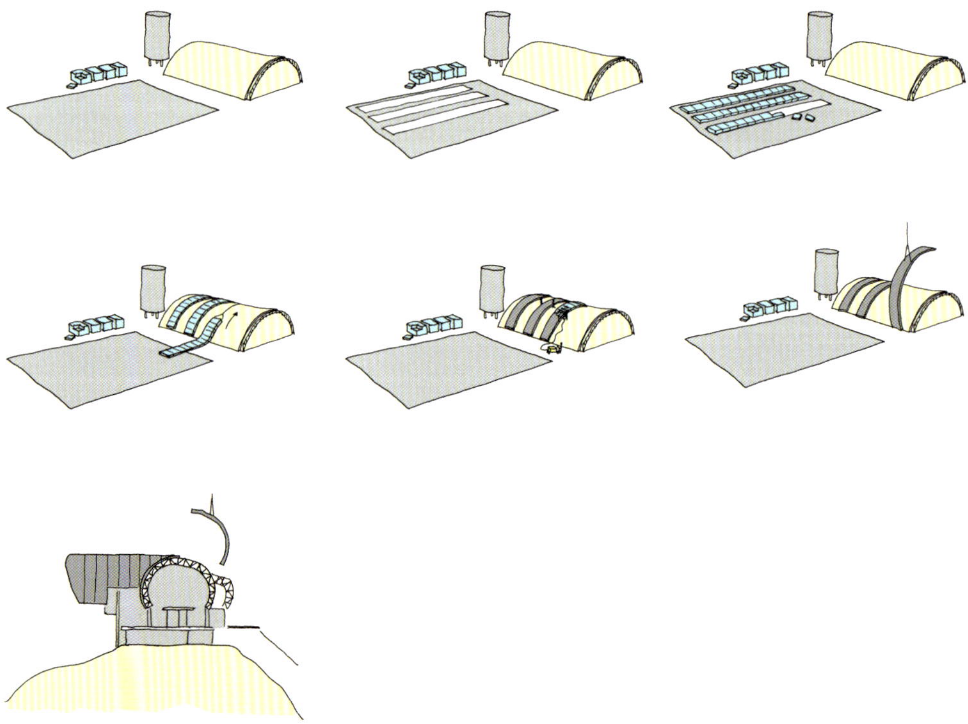

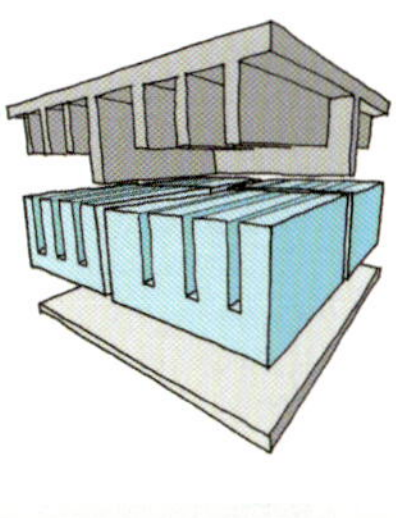
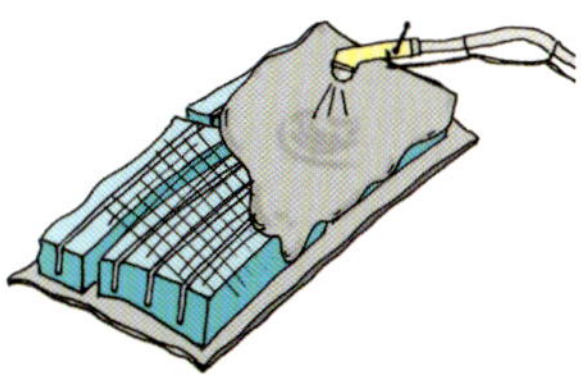
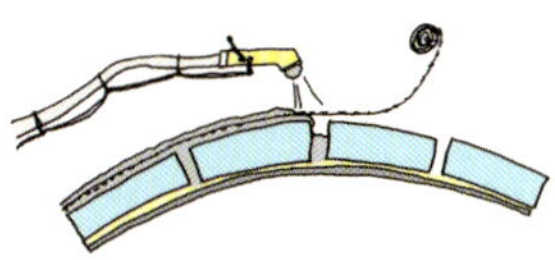

# CONCRETE VACUUM INJECTION

11-08-2007

**IMAGINED BY** M. Bilow
**KEYWORDS** structure, concrete, injection, production principle, vacuum
**PERFORMANCE** production

The basic principle of vacuum structures involves an airtight membrane enclosing pressure resistant filling elements. Upon applying vacuum, the membrane becomes stiff. This principle can be used to produce prefabricated parts.

The shipping industry offers alternative solutions: based on serial production methods, the mold is built first and then filled with the surface material and rigid foam. Polyester or epoxy is added by vacuum injection to create a sandwich composite structure.

Since there is no gravel or other coarser aggregate added to the fiber concrete matrix it can flow easily. Therefore, textile reinforcement or hollow parts can be used. One idea is to pour all dry materials into a vacuum bag and then saturate them with liquid concrete under vacuum. Prefabricated baskets with cavities and specifically arranged reinforcement fibers can thus be produced economically.

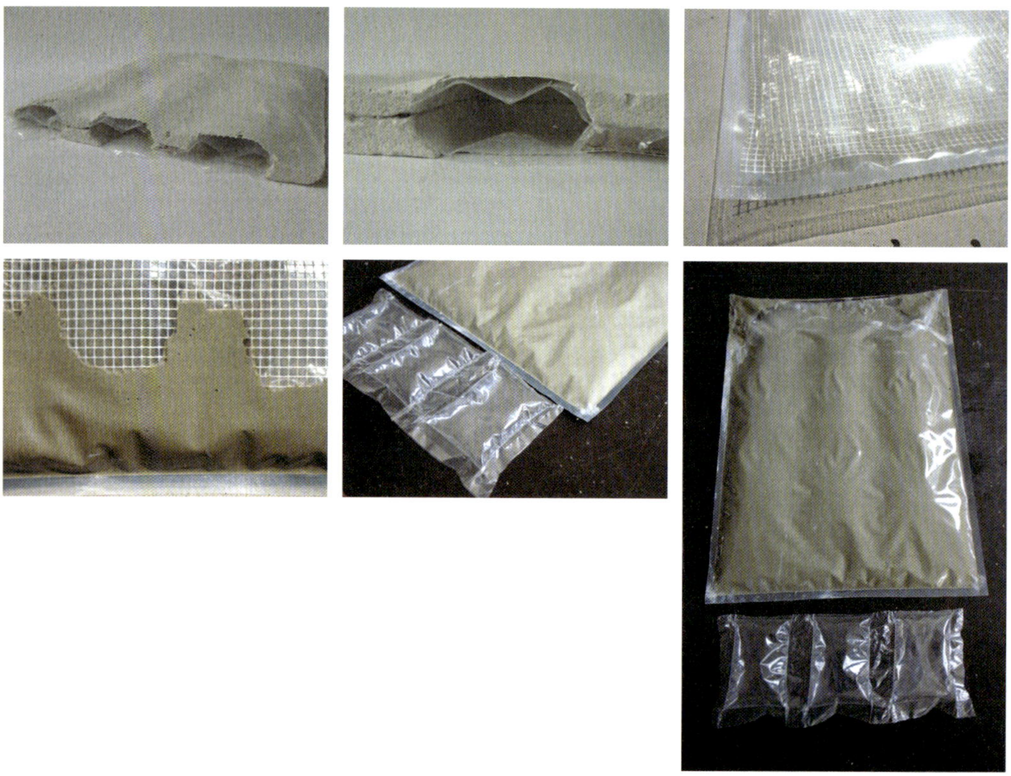

# FOAM STRUCTURE WALL

13-03-2009

**IMAGINED BY** imagine Klappergassenworkshop
**KEYWORDS** foam, structure, building material, analysis, 3D Printing
**PERFORMANCE** production

This idea for a wall structure was inspired by the appearance of lather. When individual soap bubbles in the shape of perfect spheres meet, they form a mass that is subject to geometric forces due to surface tension. If the contact areas are reinforced, the mass can be used as a structure for wall elements, for example. Suitable software programs can generate a wall element with a dense surface and a slightly porous core.
Rapid manufacturing production processes can be employed to create the wall on site or as a prefabricated building part.

SOAP BUBBLES

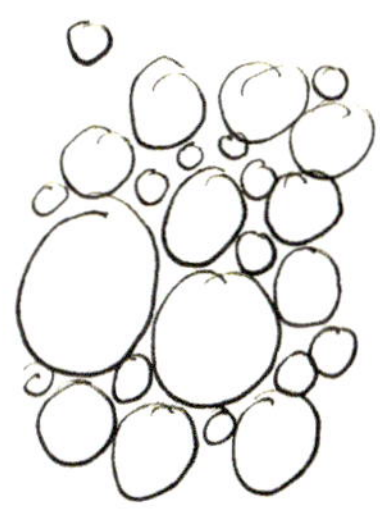

CONGLOMERATION

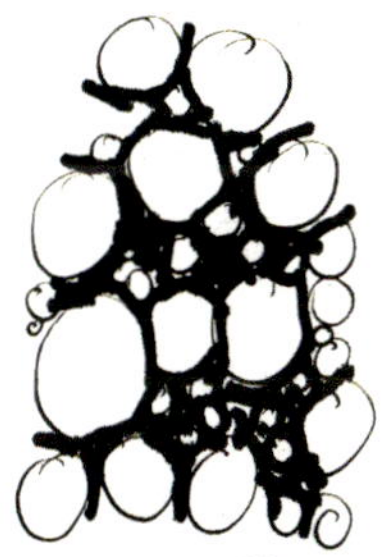

CONTACT AREAS

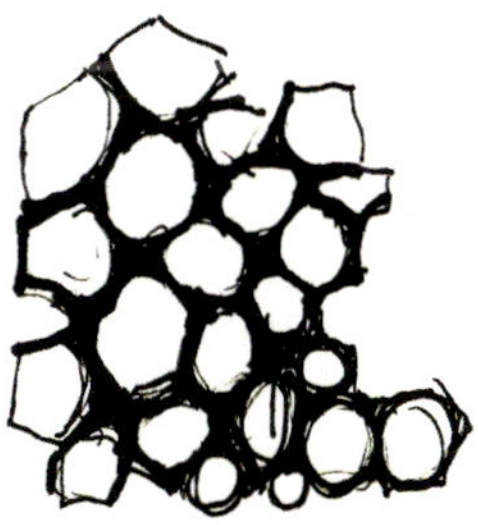

STRUCTURE ANALYSED

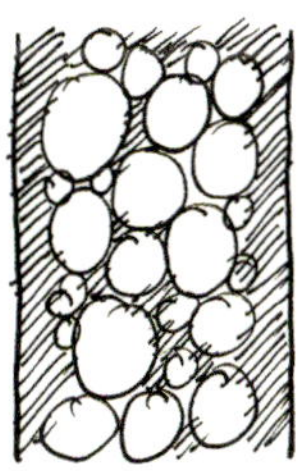

WALL ELEMENT

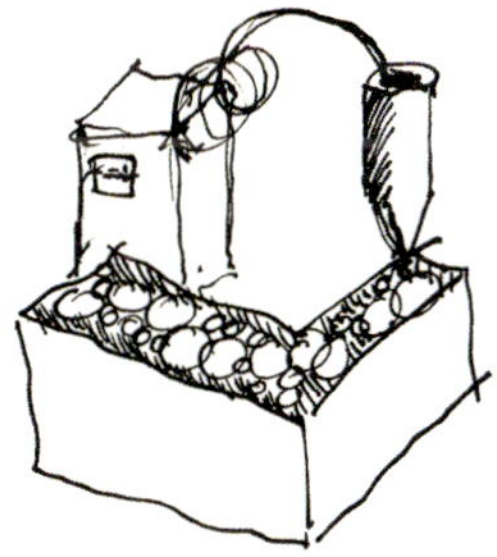

3D PRINTING

# RAMMED SALT WALL

27-10-2008

**IMAGINED BY** H. Techen, T. Auer, U. Knaack, T. Klein, M. Bilow and A. Compagno
**KEYWORDS** salt, material, dehumidification, cooling, façade
**PERFORMANCE** material

Building in humid climates like that of Abu Dhabi requires the exterior air to be dehumidified before it enters the building to provide comfortable indoor climate conditions. Its crystalline structure gives sodium chloride (common salt) hygroscopic properties; meaning it draws water. Salt is a by-product of seawater desalinization.

The concept is based on the idea to use salt in a structural as well as building physical manner to create solar-powered dehumidification in combination with natural ventilation. This would result in highly energy efficient building operation. Due to the coarse structure of its crystals, salt can be compacted layer by layer, similar to rammed earth, and can thus be formed into massive wall elements.

If used as exterior walls, the salt walls can be perforated. A glass panel installed on the outside provides protection against the weather and promotes the air in the facade gap to heat up, which in turn furthers dehumidification. Since warm air rises, it can easily be guided into the building and through the salt wall (breathing wall). Inside the wall, it can be conditioned as needed (supply air/cooled and dehumidified or exhaust air/heated and humidified).

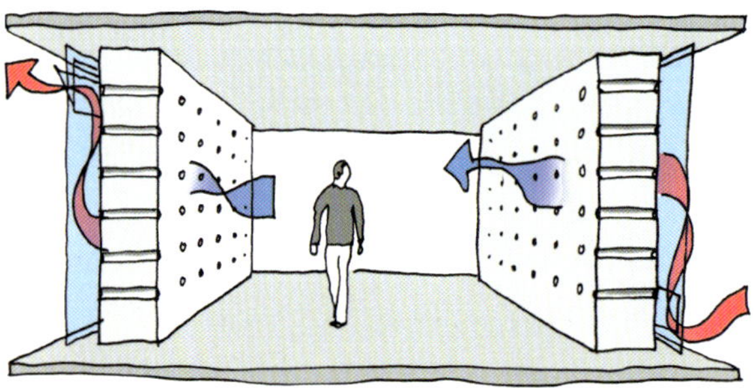

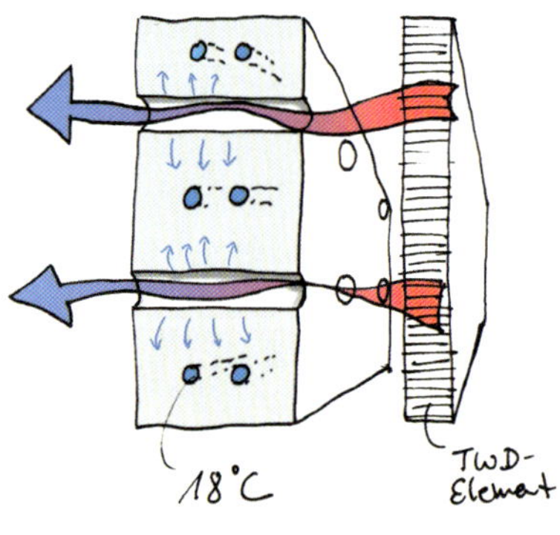

# SOLID UNITIZED WALL

26-01-2008

IMAGINED BY U. Knaack, M. Bilow
KEYWORDS façade, unitized system, structure, filling, insulation
PERFORMANCE assembly

The concept is based on the functional principle of sandwich constructions. Offset aerated concrete panels are inserted and glued into prefabricated element frames made of pultruded fiber reinforced plastics or aluminum profiles. The cover layer can be applied onto a layer of fiber concrete or other façade surface finishing. The element itself is rigid and meets all the requirements of a façade. Using element frames means simple wind and watertight joins and short construction times.

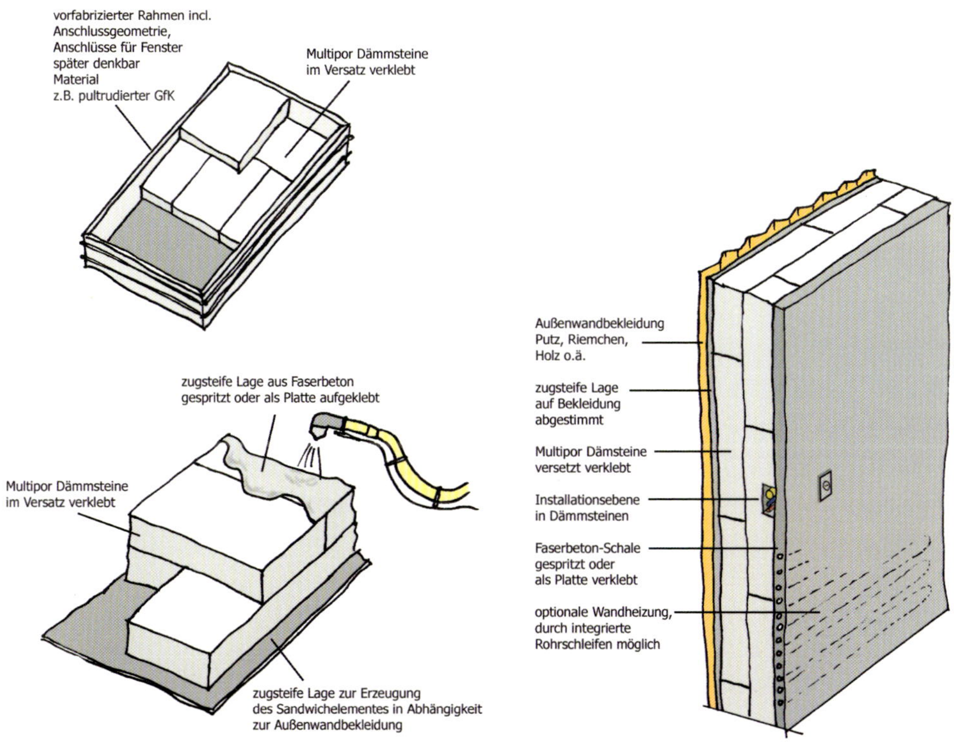

# THERMOMETRIC HOUSE

12.01.2009

IMAGINED BY Stephanie Davidson and Georg Rafailidis, supported by imagine structure and Roman Jakobiak
KEYWORDS assembly
PERFORMANCE production

The project makes use of the volume expansion during the change of phase of wax from liquid to solid and vice versa (which is usually perceived as problematic) to develop a temperature-sensitive glass block. The glass block component is not only able to increase the thermal storage capacity of a wall assembly, but is also able to define temperature-specific spaces and modulate shading and views.

We exaggerated the volume expansion and shrinkage that occurs in wax PCM by containing it in a vessel with a thermometer-like section. During volume expansion, the wax rises visibly within this cavity, acting as a sunscreen and visual screen.

But what is the spatial consequence of such a material system? While in most contemporary buildings a uniform temperature distribution is desired, we minimize the conventional temperature-controlled room to a compact core, complemented by a surrounding, spacious room perimeter, defined by an environmentally responsive thermometric façade. In this spatial arrangement, the temperature-regulating capacity of the façade offers extended time windows of thermal comfort in the generous perimeter space. The program of the core area spills into the expansive perimeter space dependent on weather and season. To avoid additional lateral bracing, the maximum running length of each wall element is 15 feet resulting in a folded façade. The folded façade creates spatial pockets with specific melting temperatures related to different programmatic activities, for example a 76 degree Fahrenheit bathroom space or a 64 degree Fahrenheit sleeping area.

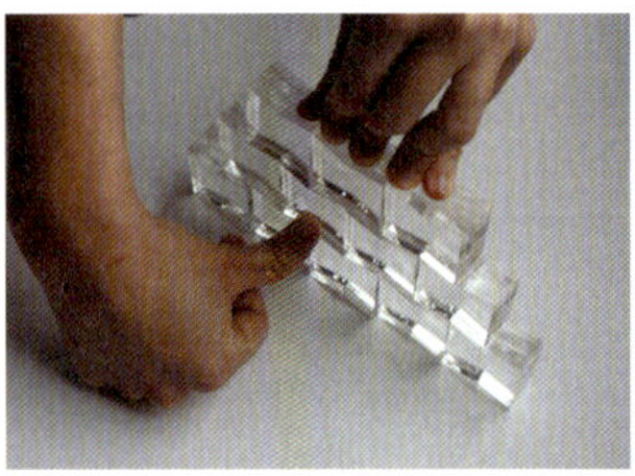
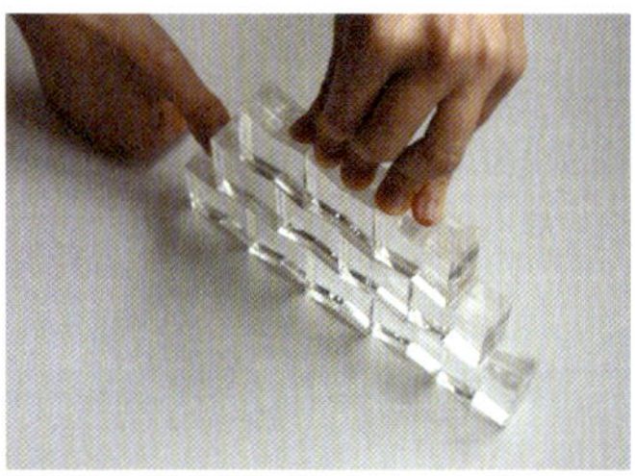
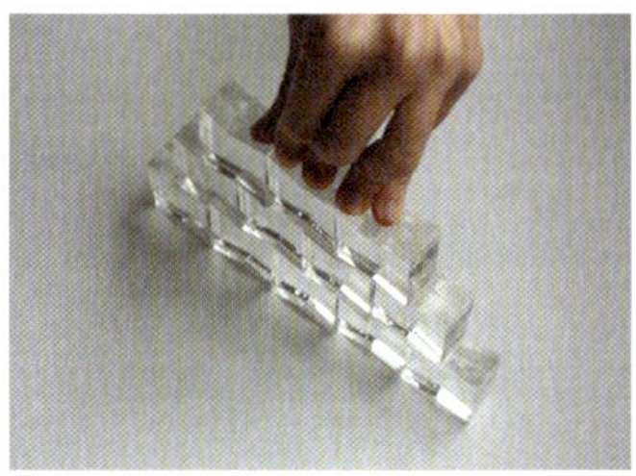

3.PARAMETER: INTERIOR GEOMETRY

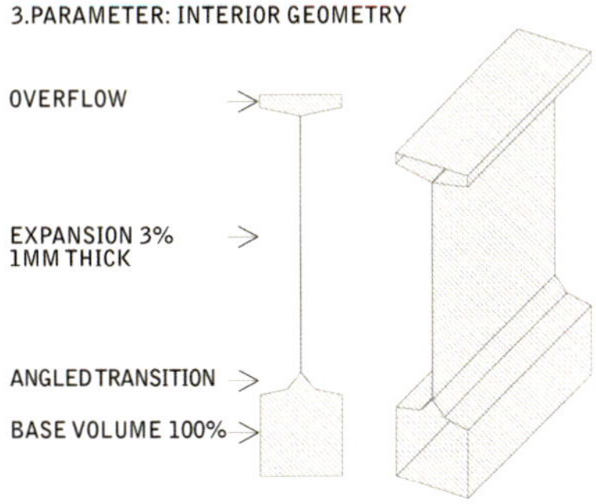


INTERIOR GEOMETRY EVOLUTION-FINAL

3.PARAMETER: INTERIOR GEOMETRY

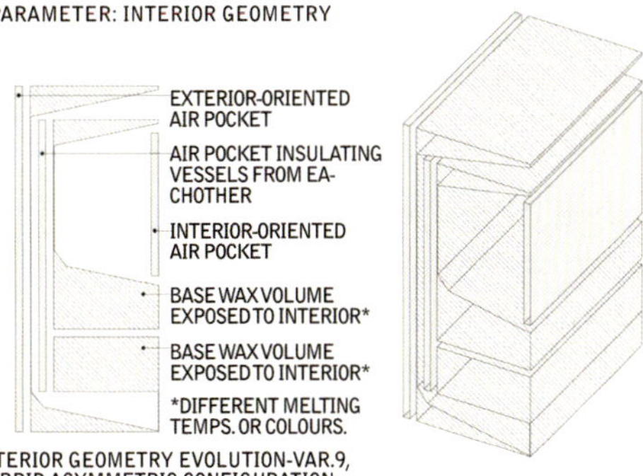


INTERIOR GEOMETRY EVOLUTION-VAR.9,
HYBRID ASYMMETRIC CONFIGURATION

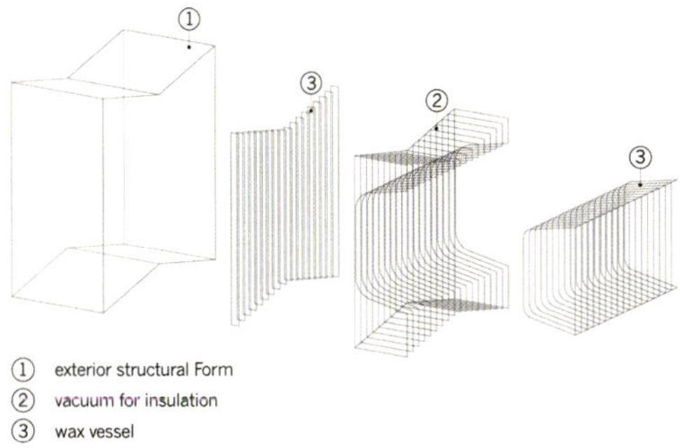


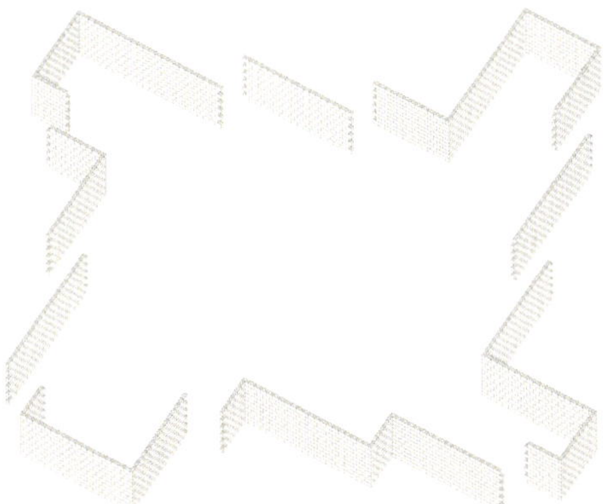

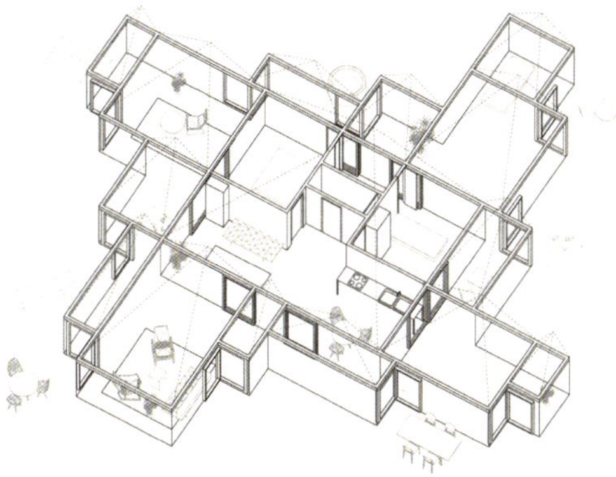

7. PARAMETER: TEMPERATURE

WALL BUILD-UP WITH BLOCKS OF VARIABLE TEMPERATURE SETTINGS

# TRI-MATERIAL CUBES

13-03-2009

IMAGINED BY imagine Klappergassenworkshop
KEYWORDS modular, system, lighting, ventilation, sun shading, load-bearing, system building, glass
PERFORMANCE assembly

Boxes consisting of three different materials form a wall that can be adapted to local conditions by turning the boxes such that a particular material faces the inside or the outside. The cubes themselves are load-bearing and form the structure of the wall. This means that the orientation of the materials which are linked to different functions is irrelevant for the stability of the construction.

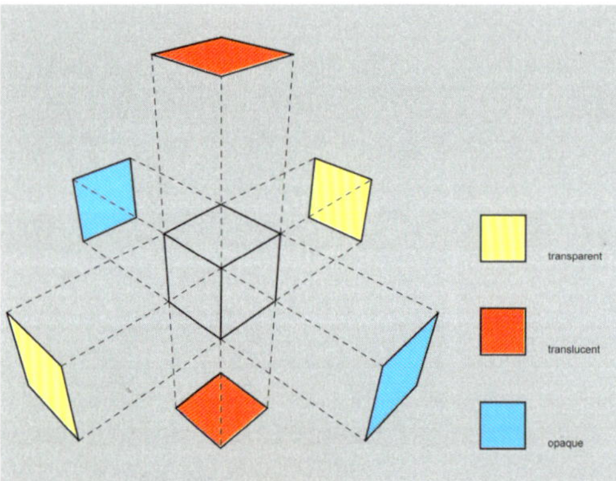


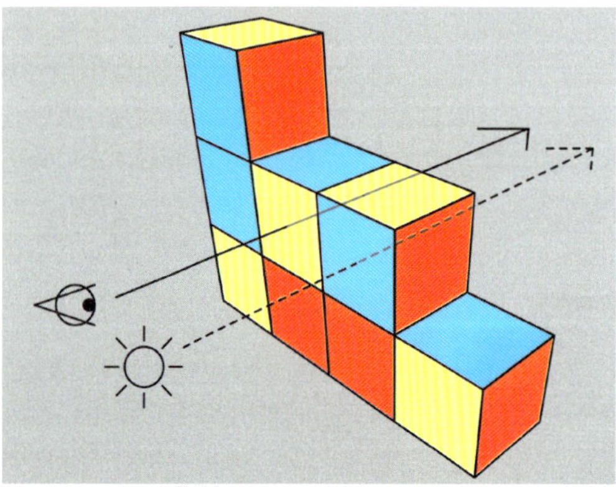

# VERTICAL GARDEN FAÇADE

06-07-2011

**IMAGINED BY** Holger Techen
**KEYWORDS** organic, insulating, energy generating
**PERFORMANCE** storage of rainwater, $CO_2$ reduction

This principle is an interesting alternative to the common, rear-ventilated brick façade; not only for refurbishment measures but also new constructions.
Weather proofing is done by applying a semi permeable seal directly onto the brickwork; the exterior wall is built with weatherproof porous concrete stones. Due to its high porosity, the stone can store precipitation water and release it to the environment time-delayed. This provides the opportunity to use the outside as a foundation for vegetation without the need for elaborate irrigation facilities. Moss or ferns and lichens can grow without substantial care. They serve as a natural climate buffer and can actively reduce $CO_2$ pollution.

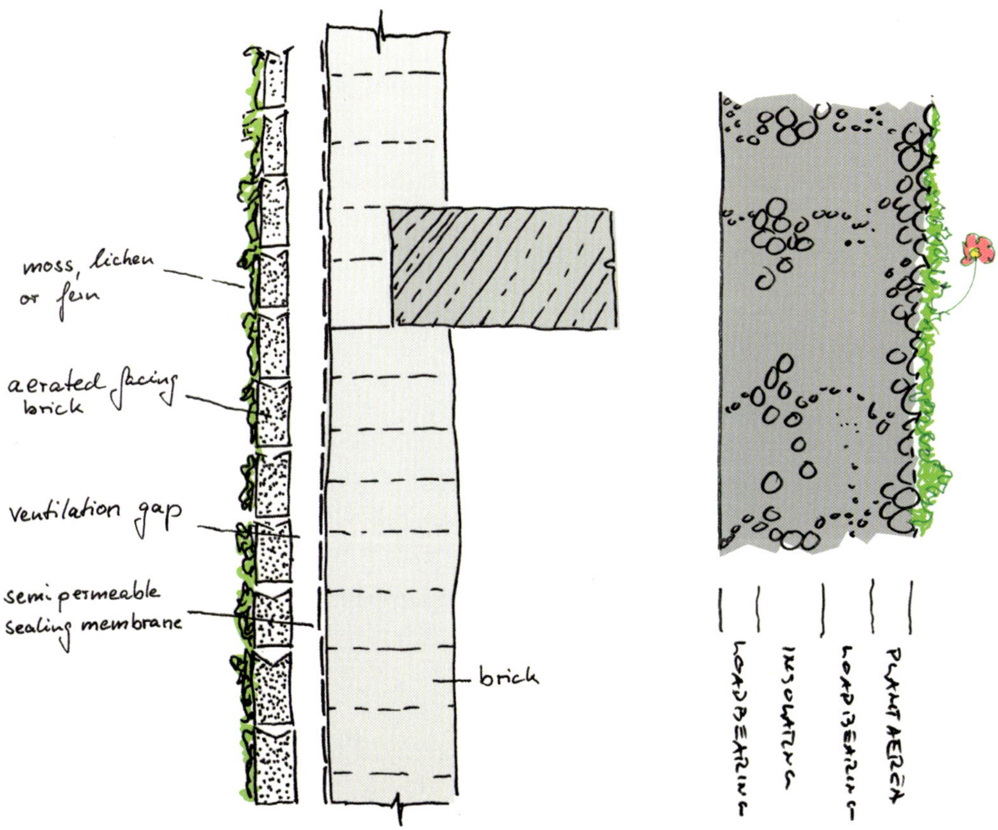

# 5. THE MASSIVE INTEGRAL WALL

# 5.1. INTEGRAL PRINCIPLE

Performance driven façades is the focus of this book – with an in-depth look at related developments. And this is where integral performance comes into play as well, with the focus lying on integration. Today's building envelope includes an increasing number of ever more complex specifications. Typically, functions such as sealing, insulating and load-bearing are layered into the façade; others such as lighting and ventilation are added via partially installed components. This transition between window and wall or load-bearing building part often poses difficulties in terms of building physics and construction. In most cases, specialized solutions are applied that might or might not be aesthetically appealing.

The integrative approach – melting together layers and specialized building parts – that we will call Integral Wall, offers numerous new options for the building envelope. It seems self-evident to interlink the functions load-bearing and insulating. The brick making industry, for example, has offered many different types of building stones for quite some time that offer load-bearing and insulating properties and therefore easily fulfill today's energy savings requirements. They can be porous, include voids or consist of a combination of insulating material and brick. However, this is not the focus of a new interpretation of the integral wall. Concrete construction also shows an increasing use of lightweight concrete with varying properties and mixtures. This type of concrete is typically used for load-bearing exterior walls. Compared with brick building, concrete building offers a larger potential to be applied to an integral wall.
The following chapter provides a short outline of the composition, manufacturing and material properties of lightweight concretes, and the potential (performance) that can be derived for the integral wall.

It seems obvious to integrate more functions into the concrete building component by either modifying the material composition or inserting ducts. The Zollverein School in Essen, Germany by SANAA has made an important contribution to this development.

Not only elements inserted into the concrete, but also modified aggregates can significantly improve insulating qualities without compromising the quality of the surface finish. Gradient materials with layers of different composition are currently tested in different research laboratories. The goal is to develop a mineral-based, pourable material that is dense in the outer layers and coarsely porous in the center by varying the material composition.
The next but one paragraph illustrates related approaches in more detail, and describes technology transfer to develop gradients for other materials.

But what can we derive for other principles/concepts? Further material development in the building industry itself, but also the use of materials and their implementation in the building environment, is mostly ignored.
Another parallel and deciding factor is manufacturing and assembly methods. Which technologies are currently available for on-site construction or

1

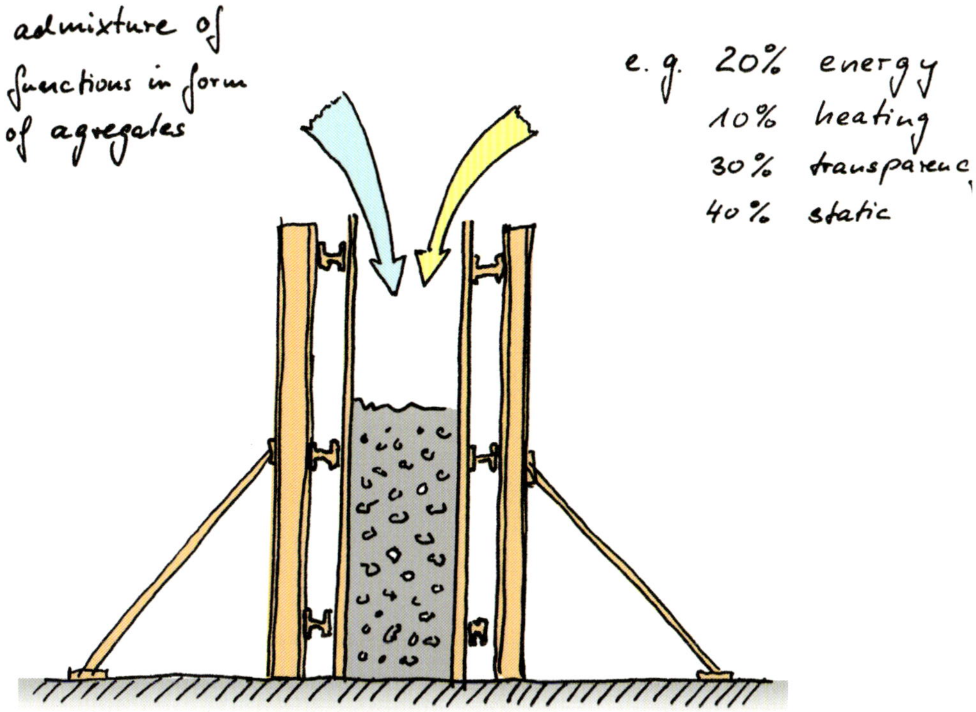


2

3

1 Basic scheme of material composition
2 Design School Essen
3 Design School Essen, interior with acoustic and sunscreen curtain

have the potential to be used in combination with other materials? How can we exploit manufacturing technologies from other disciplines for serial production of new integrated façade elements? Is there, for example, a vision of "Performance Driven Mixture"? Will there be a time when individual aggregates can be selected in accordance with particular functions of the building envelope to mix a new material exactly adapted to a particular application?

The "Integral Principals" introduced in the following pages are conceptual ideas in response to these questions.

# 5.2. A SAMPLE IN CONCRETE – THE INTEGRAL MASSIVE WALL

## INITIAL SITUATION

Currently, linking multiple functions in an exterior wall can be most efficiently done by using mineral materials. Building stones and lightweight concrete are particularly noteworthy in this context. To facilitate an understanding of the subject of integral massive walls, we will begin by providing a short overview of the status quo.

Concrete can be divided into numerous classifications. For our purpose, the different types of lightweight concrete and their properties are of particular interest.

Lightweight concrete comes in many different forms: porous lightweight concrete with a compact crystalline structure, air-entrained lightweight concrete, lightweight concrete with open structure (with compact or porous mineral aggregate), and air-entrained concrete.

These types of concrete differ in terms of their ingredients, production methods, material and processing properties; thus providing interesting potential for the development of new composite materials.

## POROUS LIGHTWEIGHT CONCRETE WITH A COMPACT CRYSTALLINE STRUCTURE

The material composition of this type of concrete, also called lightweight construction concrete, largely corresponds to that of regular concrete. Aggregates such as gravel or crushed rock are replaced by light mineral aggregates with low densities (800 – 2000 kg/m$^3$). Cavities are filled with cement paste. Due to this great variety, lightweight concrete is classified in classes of density. Firmness and durability of lightweight construction concrete is comparable to that of regular concrete. However, in part its elasticity modulus differs greatly from that of normal concrete. Weight reduction is achieved by adding aggregates such as expanded clay, foam glass, expanded shale or natural pumice. Expansion, i.e. multiple enlargement of the original particle size, is achieved by sintering the raw materials in rotary furnaces. During this burning process, a sintered skin is formed around the expanded particles, responsible for strength and density.
On the other hand, the sintering skin has a negative effect on the particle weight, i.e. the density of the expanded particles. The sintered skin covers the entire expanded aggregate particles and thus reduces water absorption. It seals the aggregate. This in turn influences the water-cement ratio which is a determining factor for the toughness and processability of concrete.

Lightweight concretes are weaker than regular concrete, resulting from a lower compression strength of the light aggregate. Whereas compression strength and elasticity modulus of regular concrete depend on the cement stone, with lightweight concrete they are solely influenced by the toughness of the aggregate. The load-bearing capacity of lightweight concrete is based on a different mechanical model. Due to their low strength, lightweight aggregates loose load-bearing performance with increasing loads. They can only improve the stiffness of the cement paste which therefore takes on the load-bearing and strengthening function.

The correlation between water-cement ratio and compression strength is only partially valid for lightweight concrete.

1 Clay structure
2 Natural stone masonry
3 Brick wall
4 Concrete cast in wooden formwork
5 Exposed aggregate concrete
6 Glass fiber reinforced concrete (Durapact Haan – Germany)

7

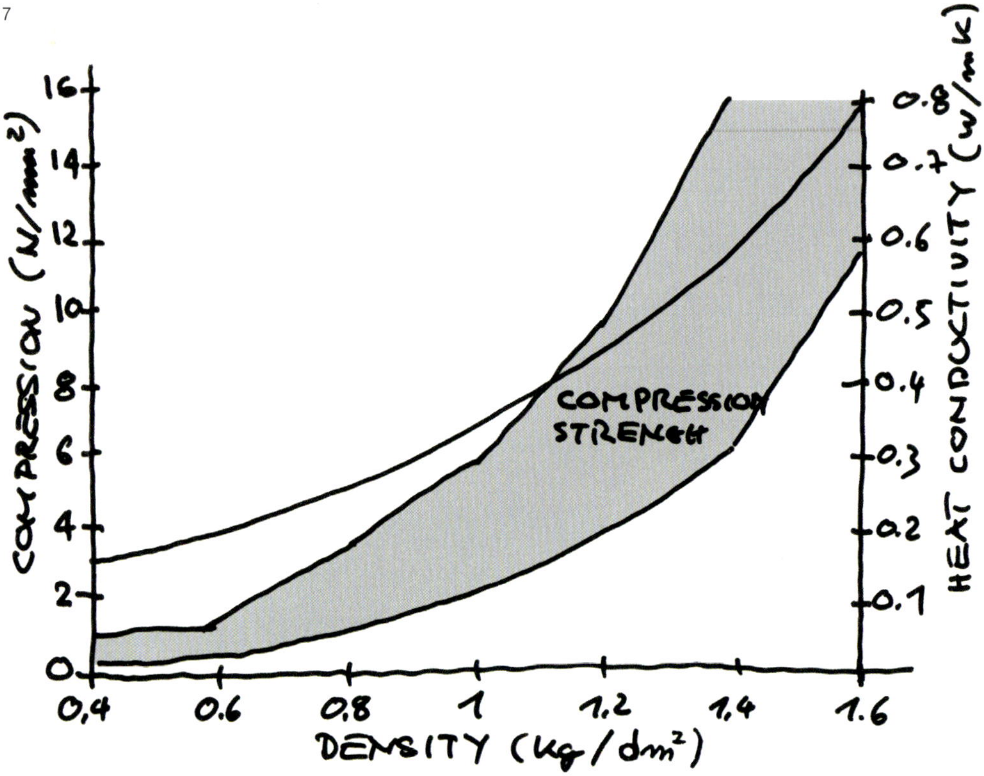

7 Properties of air-entrained lightweight concrete
8 Lightweight concrete
9 Close-up of lightweight concrete

Higher strengths can only be achieved by higher density, which, however, has a negative effect on the heat insulation properties of lightweight concrete.

## AIR-ENTRAINED LIGHTWEIGHT CONCRETE

The main differentiation between air-entrained lightweight concrete and regular lightweight concrete is its lower density and the resulting higher insulation properties. To produce air-entrained lightweight concrete, foam is made in a foaming device from a foaming agent and water. Then, small amounts of mortar or concrete are added. Often, air-entraining agents are used to increase the porosity of the aerated concrete. The aggregates added can be dense or porous. Density values of as low as 400 kg/m$^3$ can be reached with highly porous aggregates.

Due to its high ratio of entrained air, this lightweight concrete requires general technical approval if used as a load-bearing element.

## LIGHTWEIGHT CONCRETE WITH OPEN STRUCTURE

The composition of lightweight concrete with open structure is also focused on a large ratio of pores. The amount of cement paste used is reduced such that the aggregate is merely coated and only pointwise connected. Compared to air-entrained lightweight concrete, this method can achieve an even higher porosity. Typically, lightweight concrete with open structure is a single-sized concrete and is currently used for non load-bearing prefabricated parts, building stones or other secondary building components. Just as with lightweight concrete, the porous mineral aggregates consist of expanded clay, expanded shale, or natural pumice. Lightweight concrete with open structure can achieve heat conductivity values comparable to those of wood. Compression strength of between 2 and 20 MPa is far lower than that of regular concrete. Therefore it is not suited for pillars, ceilings, joists, etc.

With this type of lightweight concrete, low strength and elasticity modulus result in a higher risk of shrinkage cracks, which can only be counteracted by limiting the component dimensions.

## POROUS CONCRETE

Porous concrete features a mostly closed-celled structure with pores between 0.5 and 1.5 mm. It is typically used for light wall panels, building stones and small boards. Porous concrete consists of finely ground quartz sand, quick lime, cement, and water. Pore intensity is regulated by the amount of aluminum powder added. Porous concrete is predominantly used as a non reinforced building material. It can be cut after stiffening. Its maximum compression strength of 8 MPa is only reached after 6 – 12 hours in an autoclave at 190° C and a pressure of 12 bar. Corresponding to density values between 350 and 1,000 kg/m$^3$, porous concrete has a heat conductivity of only 0.09 W/$^3$ K.

This overview of different types of lightweight concrete shows the degree to which the composition of the ingredients alone can have significant influence on its compression strength and density, but particularly on the heat insulating properties of a mineral material. It is intended to demonstrate the potential of mineral materials for an application in an integral wall.

# 5.3. SOME ASPECTS OF GRADIENT MATERIALS

A gradient material can be understood as a multiphase system featuring location-dependent, physical, chemical or mechanical properties. Gradation, i.e. a change of material properties as a multiphase process across the thickness of an element, can be efficiently used to exploit certain properties of a material or to mix different materials to adapt to specific requirements.

In the building industry, gradient materials can be used to optimize the mechanical and building physical properties of a building component. Gradient materials can feature a continuous change in property or a stepped change across their cross section. In relation to mineral products such as cement, concrete, lime, and clay, different degrees of porosity, density and fiber content as well as the ratio of components can be used to create property gradation.

A continuous phase change can minimize building-physical weaknesses and adapt thermal insulation properties to a specific requirement in the building. Naturally, mechanical properties and thermal expansion coefficients can be thus regulated as well.

Current approaches to realize these developments are only applied to small building parts.

Manufacturing methods and possible property optimization of gradient materials vary with the materials selected (mineral materials, metals, polymers, textiles). Whereas manufacturing methods already exist to produce gradient materials from polymers and metals and these materials are already applied in electronics or the chemical industry, developments to use gradient mineral materials in the building industry are still in their infancy. Gradient materials offer alternative solutions for the building industry and the building envelope in particular. Interesting development potential results not only from the possibility to control thermal insulation properties by using different element thicknesses but also from a reduction in material quantity and $CO_2$ emission.

As previously explained in the section about different types of lightweight concrete, a variation in porosity and aggregate can be used to control density, heat insulation capacity and rigidity. Today, lightweight concretes feature heat insulation values comparable to those of open-celled foam materials.

A variation of these extreme lightweight concretes with dense and load-bearing outer layers on the inside and outside of an element is an important goal to be developed. Several universities and testing facilities are currently working on varying all available concrete aggregates.

With foams/insulation materials, certain gradation methods can be used to create a continuous progression from open-celled to closed-celled structures. Such continuous gradation in material porosity can be achieved by infiltrating a second material into the foam. However, in the field of fabricating insulation materials, this technology is still at the very beginning. Gradient textiles offer benefits for controlling material stiffness/expansion behavior and fiber density. Such fluent progression from one material to another can be accomplished by modifying existing manufacturing methods.

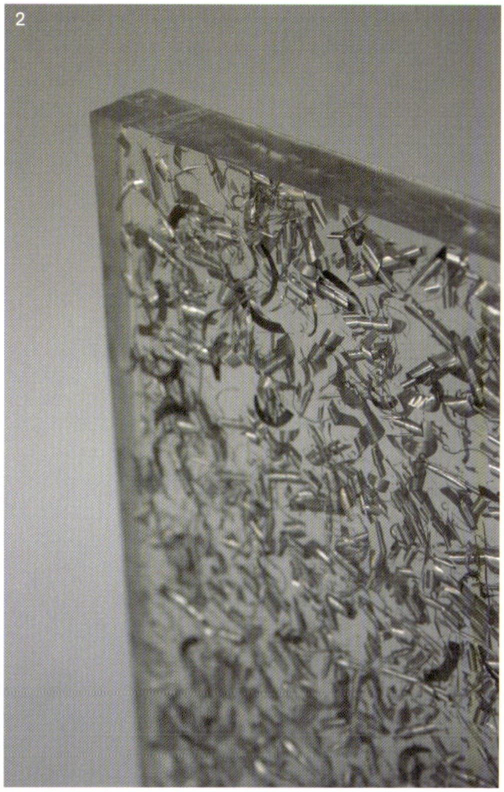

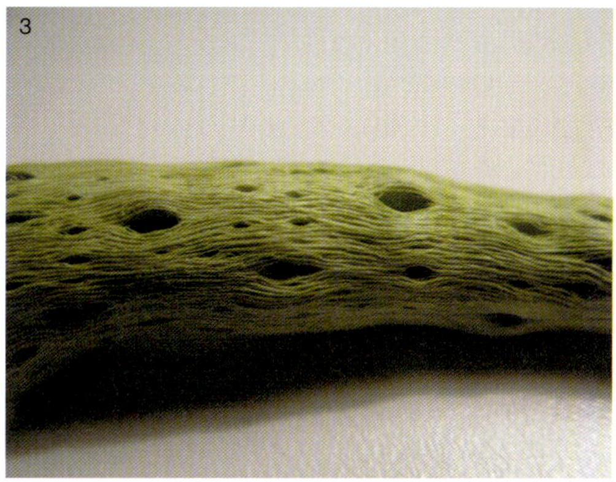

1 Composite and sandwich 1
2 Metal chips in cast resin as a composite
3 Wood fibers as a natural composite

In the field of metals, we can already mix different metals, as well as metals with ceramics, under high temperature and pressure to exploit the advantages of a particular alloy. As with mixing two different metals, producing metal-ceramics materials always raises the question as to whether the thermal expansion coefficients of the two or more materials are compatible.

Combining metals and ceramics leads to particularly exciting new applications. The thermomechanical behavior of the composite material can be optimized through the material properties of the individual ingredients, and content parameters such as volumetric content and matricity. It is not so much the heat insulation properties that stand in the foreground of such graded metal ceramics materials, but rather an optimization of the thermal expansion coefficient and stress-strain behavior.

The thermomechanical behavior of these 2-phase composites is determined by the volume share as well as the interpenetration of the two phases. The interpenetration of the individual materials is generally called matrix character; it describes the volume share of the individual ingredients.

The matrix character can control the stress-strain properties (mechanical properties), as can be seen in the diagram below. This creates entirely new possibilities for targeted changes in the mechanical properties of metals for applications in the building industry.

Completely new fabrication methods, derived from traditional polymer production methods, were developed for gradient materials based on duromer or thermoplastic polymers.

Gradient materials can be produced by changing the sequence of different material layers as well as by combining different grain fractions or types of grain to achieve a continuous progression of the material properties within one polymer building part.

Viscosity and the content share of a thixotropic agent have a strong influence on a gradient polymer material. The more thixotropic agent, the higher the system's viscosity. But grain parameters such as density, grain shape and size impact on viscosity.

These three parameters influence the transition from a continuously homogenous material to a gradient material to complete sedimentation, i.e. a separation of the individual materials/ingredients into layers. Contrary to the options described previously for other materials, these polymer properties are decisive for the fabrication process, which is typically done with centrifuges. Input parameters can be used to show the centrifuge parameters such as time and rotating speed with increasing viscosity. This means that for fabrication, five essential parameters need to be matched. They are determined by the composition of the polymer (grain characteristics, thixotropic agent content and achievable viscosity), as well as by production parameters of the centrifuge such as duration and rotation. In summary this means that using graded thermoplastics involves many more challenges than those of graded mineral or metal materials because the number of relevant parameters of the latter is far smaller.

LITERATURE

Mikromechanische Modellierung des mechanischen Verhaltensvon Metall/Keramik-Gradientenwerkstoffen; DFG-Projekt Schm-746/12-1 und 12/2; BA-Nr 1161/1185.

Pulvergefüllte Gradientenwerkstoffe durch Zentrifugation: Dissertation Lars Peters, Fakultät für Bergbau, Hüttenbau und Maschienenwesen der TU Clausthal – 2004.

4

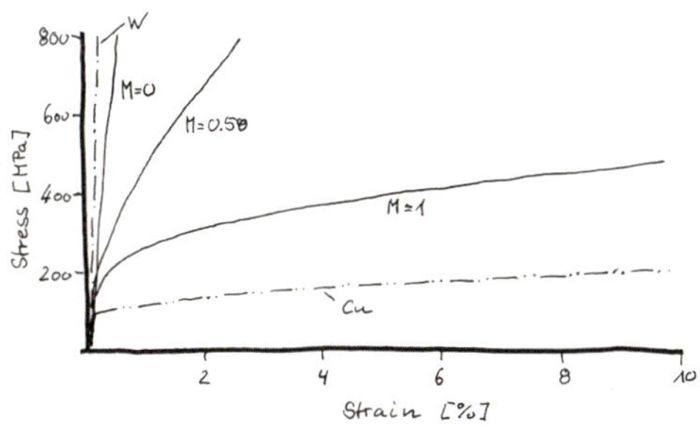


5

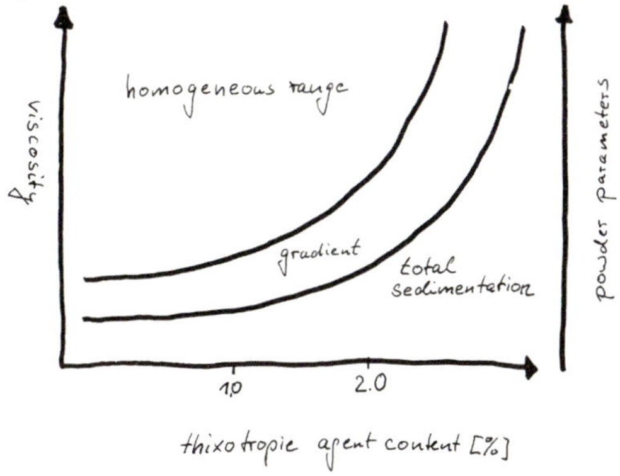


6

7

8

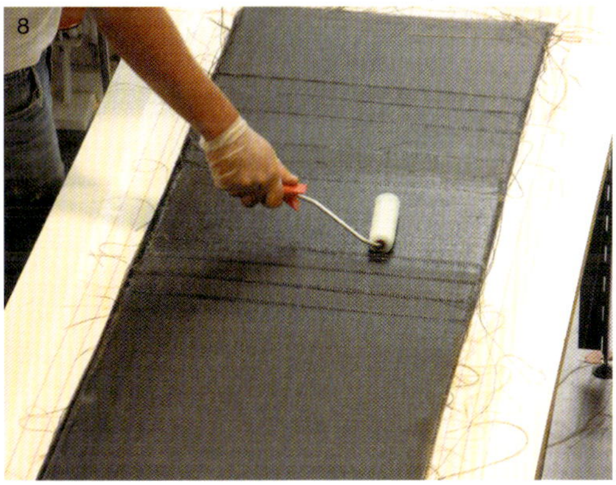

4 Influence of the matrix character M on the stress-strain behavior of a wolfram / copper compound
5 Processing window in dependence of thixotropy and viscosity
6 Hole pattern – gradient material
7 Chocolate bar – alternating gradient material
8 Gradient material laminate – stepped gradient material

# 5.4. INTEGRAL PRINCIPLES

# ACTIVE CAVITY WALL ELEMENT

04-07-2011

**IMAGINED BY** Holger Techen
**KEYWORDS** double filigree wall system, insulating concrete matrix, heating/cooling pipes
**PERFORMANCE** function integration

Further development of the cavity wall element, consisting of two filigree panels with spacing reinforcement made of stainless steel. The filigree elements are created based on a traditional manufacturing process. Only the heating/cooling pipes are prefabricated and are installed element by element prior to mounting the filigree panel. Thus, each cavity wall element has its own heating/cooling system which is connected to the general circuit upon completion of the installation. If the elements consist of lightweight concrete, there is no need for additional thermal insulation. Only the connection between the filigree panels and the lightweight concrete elements needs to be modified.

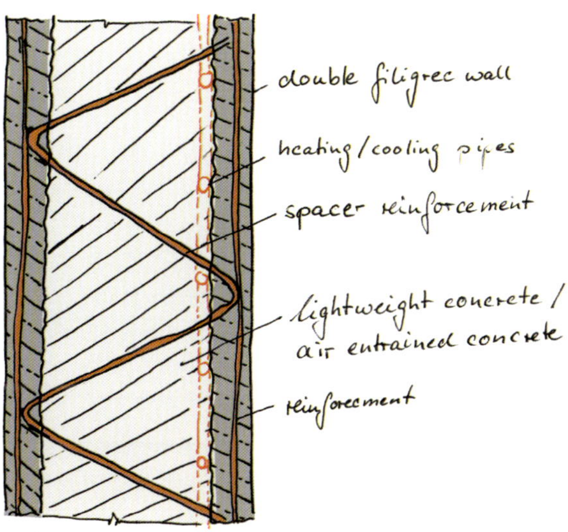


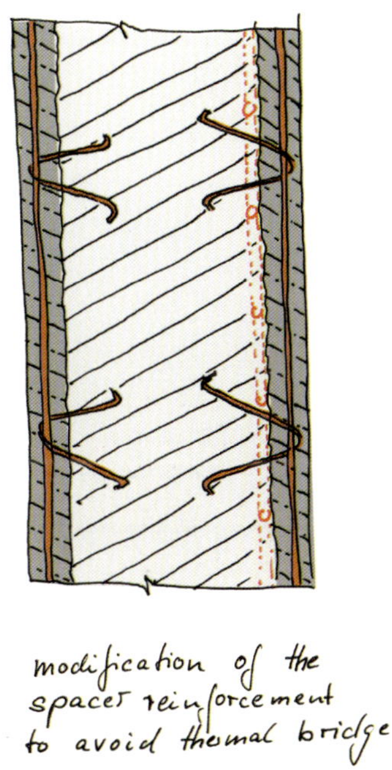

# COMPONENT FAÇADE

18-05-2009

**IMAGINED BY** Leonie van Ginkel, guided by T. Klein
**KEYWORDS** prefabricated, modular, ventilating, heating, cooling, adapting, envelope, aluminum, plastics, composites
**PERFORMANCE** assembly

This scenario is based on the idea that the façade itself does not have an independent load-bearing structure but consists of equally shaped interconnected components. The results of a form study showed that the optimum shape for such a component is a hexagon. In nature, we find hexagons in honeycomb structures that contain maximum amounts of honey with minimal amounts of beeswax.
The assignment of the functions and components is described in a diagram. In a simplified manner, the diagram shows the assignment of a selection of functions to components, and the interfaces between them. In principle, each of the components can fulfill a different function. All of them, however, fulfill the structural function.

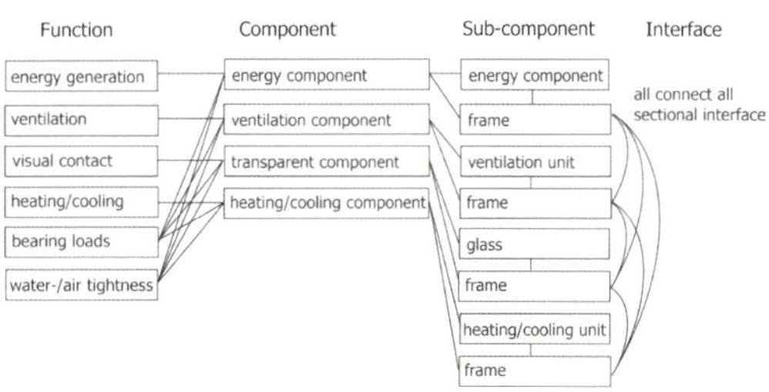

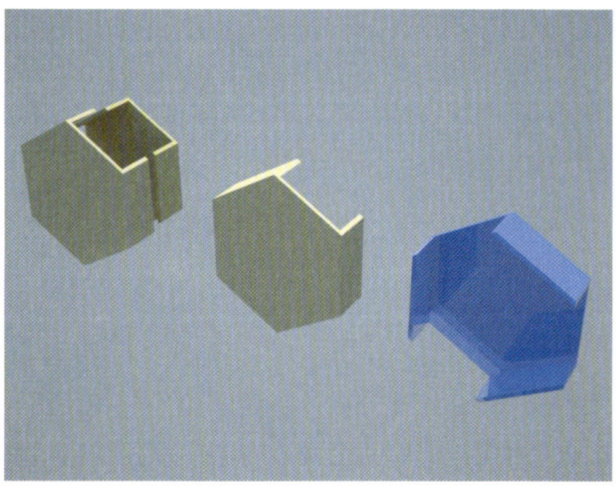

## Component shape

Transport

| | | | | |
|---|---|---|---|---|
| Replacement | No substructure | Substructure | No substructure | Substructure |
| Stability | + | - | + | - |
| Architecture | Neutral | Specific | Specific | Specific |

Network

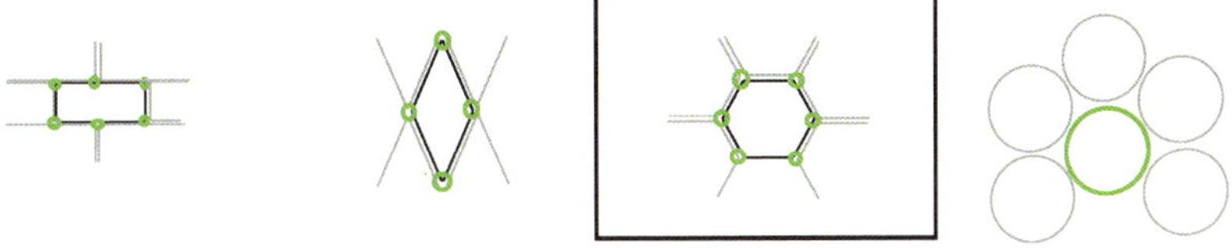

Detail connection

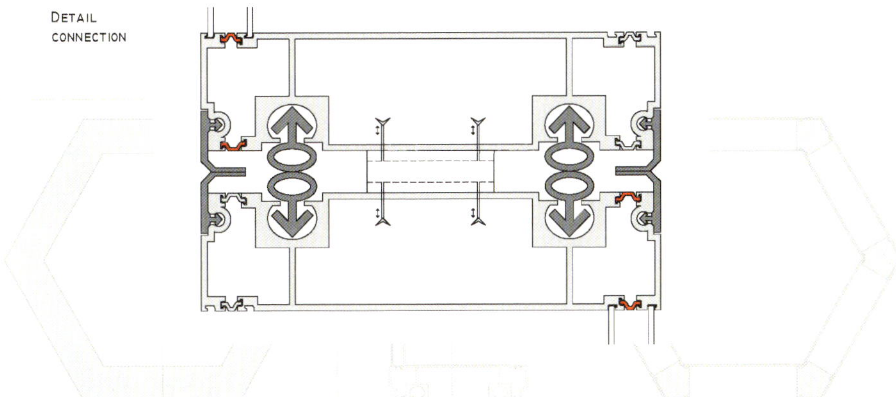

Detail connection

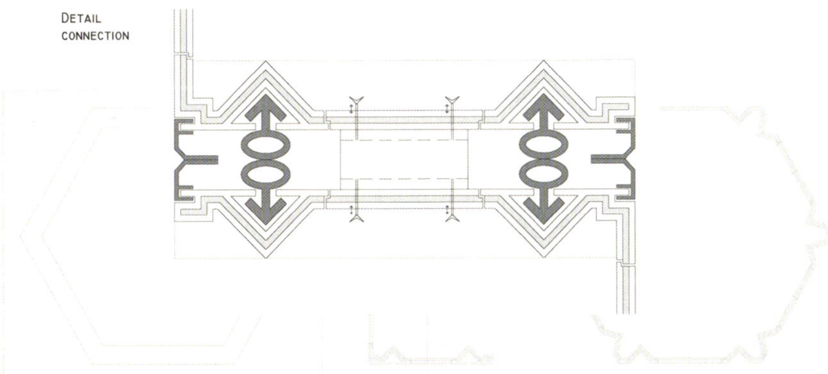

# CONCRETE MATTRESS

06-07-2011

**IMAGINED BY** Holger Techen
**KEYWORDS** spacing fabrics, lightweight concrete, prefabricated concrete elements, surface texture, embedded functional filigrees
**PERFORMANCE** integration of different functions

Spacing fabrics are used to fulfill two different functions; as a flexible formwork and to produce a specific surface texture. Two pieces of fabric are tailored with all necessary connecting filaments for distance and grid. The pieces are placed and tightened in a frame in order to fill the created space with lightweight concrete or air-entrained concrete. The spacing filaments are used for sensors, light conductors or daylight transmitters. Lightweight concrete provides thermal insulation. Surface texture and geometry is influenced by the choice of fabric.

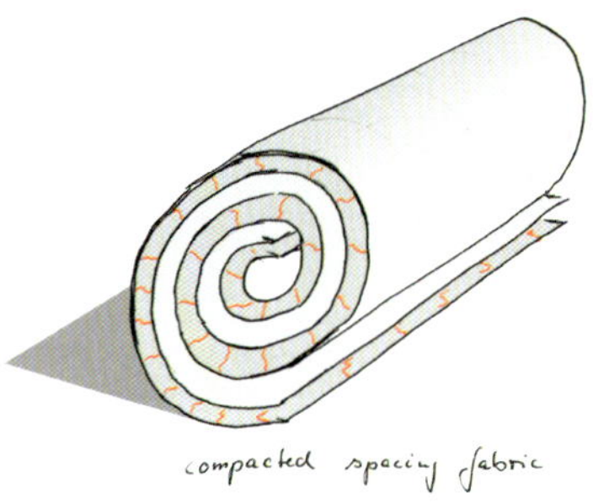


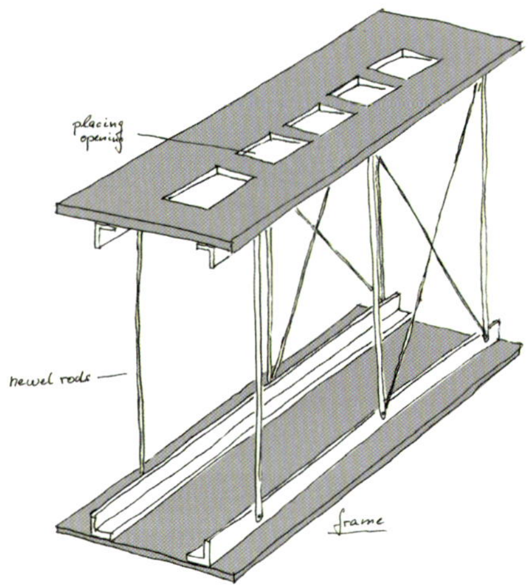


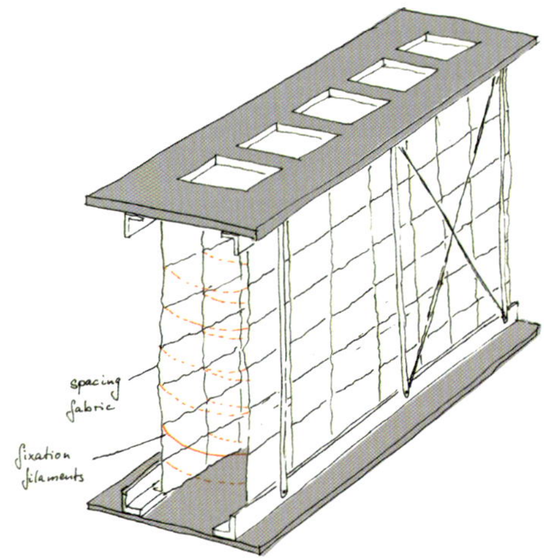


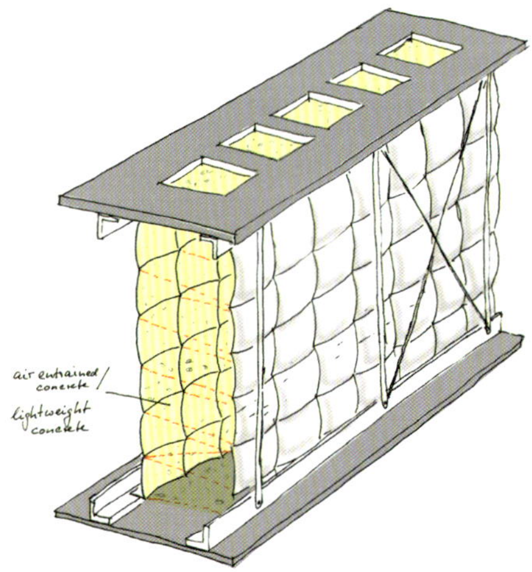

# INSULATED FLOOR–FAÇADE CONNECTION

04-07-2011

IMAGINED BY Holger Techen
KEYWORDS concrete skeleton construction, cast-in-situ, insulating concrete matrix, performance, integral façade
PERFORMANCE combination of standardized and preformed systems

This principle focuses on the border area of a classic reinforced concrete slab. If the design includes integral walls, the ceiling border is a critical area in building-physical terms that requires extra attention. Using lightweight concrete significantly improves the insulation properties in the border area and thus eliminates the need for additional insulation on the side of the ceiling facing outward.

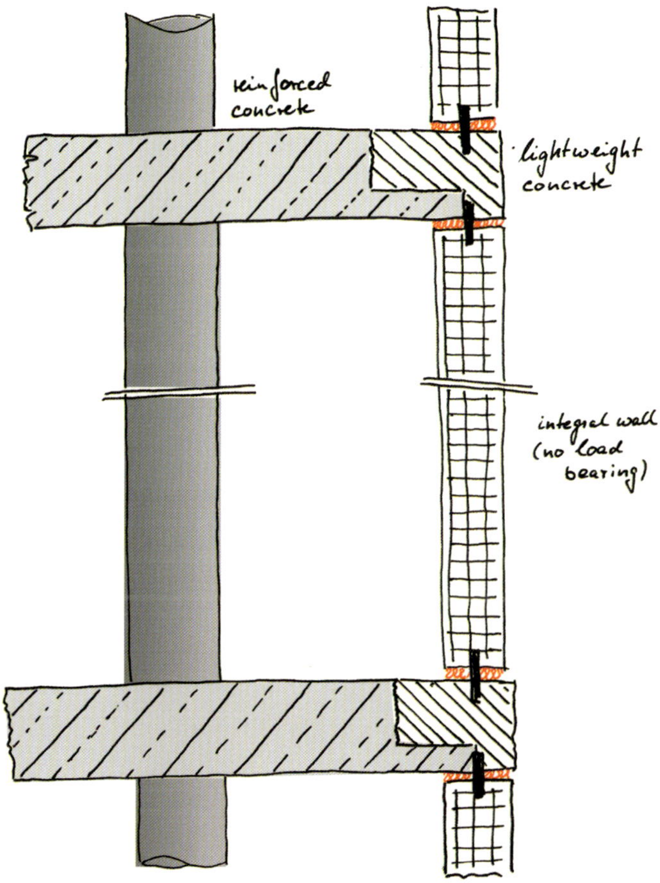

# INTEGRAL WALL

18-05-2009

**IMAGINED BY** Charlotte Heesbeen, guided by T. Klein
**KEYWORDS** composite, free-form, ventilating, heating, cooling, load bearing, solid, envelope, unknown material
**PERFORMANCE** integrated functions

This approach can be explained with the example of a tea cup. In the first cup, each main function is translated into a separate component. The second cup shows an integral architecture. But what does an integral approach mean for façade construction?
The source of inspiration for this principle is the structure of bones. Basically, the entire bone is made from one material – tissue – but different zones comprise different types of tissue to serve different functions. The outer cartilage is soft and ductile and protects the actual bone structure. This is divided into a very massive and a sponge-like structure to minimize weight.
Transferred to material science and architecture this means that an integral material could be influenced in order to achieve different functionality. Mass and porosity can influence the structure as well as the insulation properties of a material. For other functions, the shape can be adjusted or additives, such as embedded reflective elements, can be used to create an enhancing effect.
The façade design is based on these aspects. Mass is accumulated where it is needed for the structure of the building. For insulation purposes, the outer area is porous. Continuous pores in the inner area can transport warm and cold water. Embedded glass fibers transport light.
The benefit of an integral design is potentially higher performance, because the product can be adjusted according to its functionality. Standard interfaces are always based on compromises. But with an integral approach there is no need for physical interfaces between different functional components; the concept is based on seamless construction with its many benefits. On the other hand, the façade cannot be adapted at a later stage and integral constructions have an influence on the ability to recycle. In order to achieve some degree of adaptability, interfaces have to be introduced to connect components that need to be exchanged. Additional features can be used to create a modular interface, such as an integrated nut into which a bolt can be mounted to attach more functional components.
The design shows that integral product architecture requires integral design and integral production facilities.

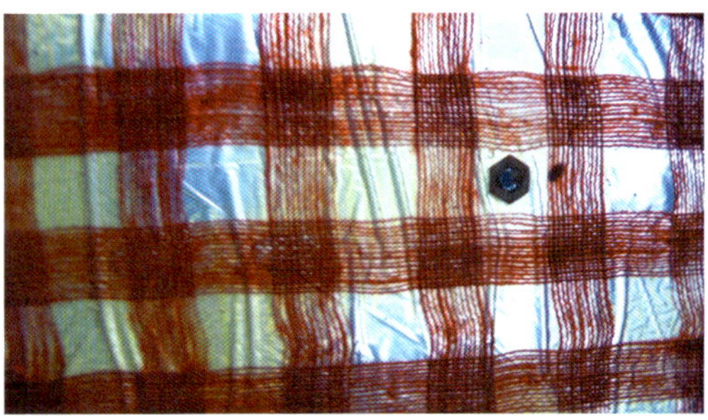

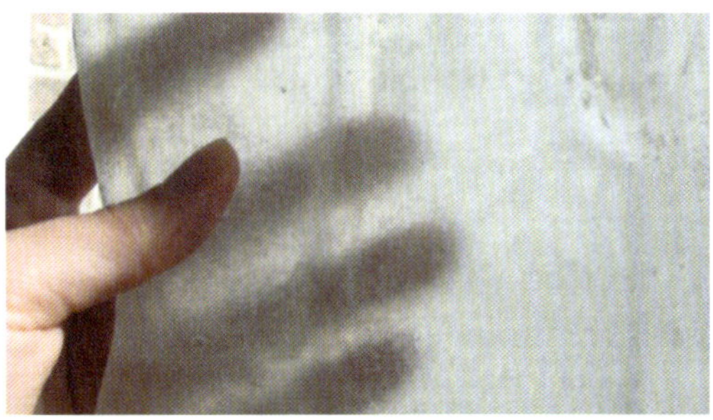

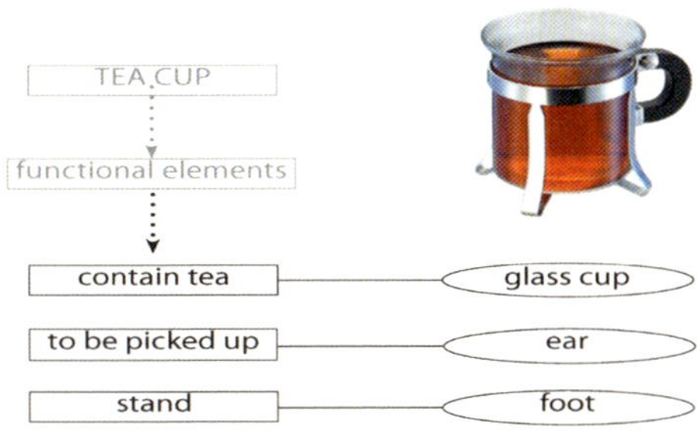
TEA CUP
functional elements
contain tea
to be picked up
stand
glass cup
ear
foot

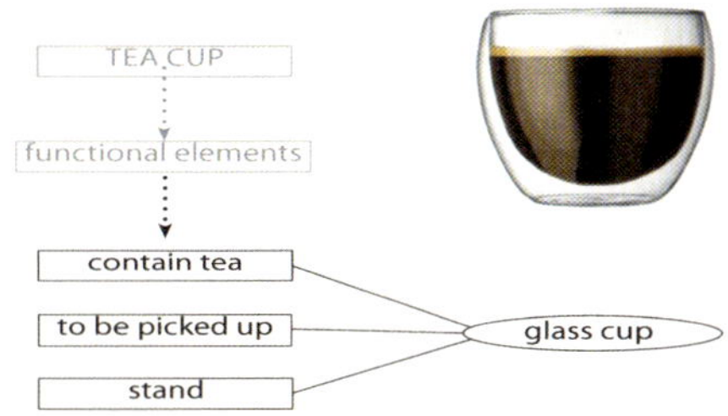
TEA CUP
functional elements
contain tea
to be picked up
stand
glass cup

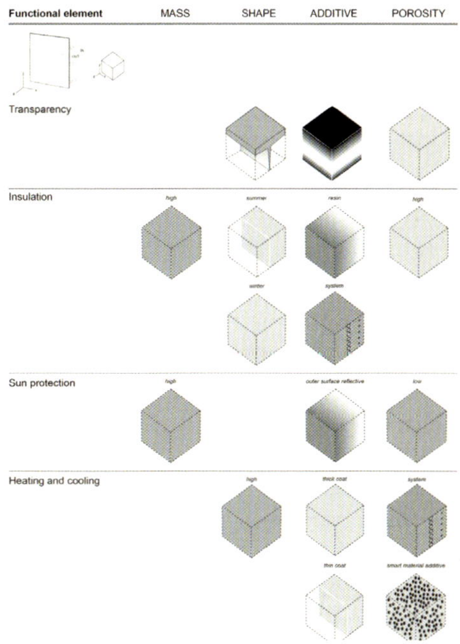
Functional element
MASS
SHAPE
ADDITIVE
POROSITY
Transparency
Insulation
Sun protection
Heating and cooling

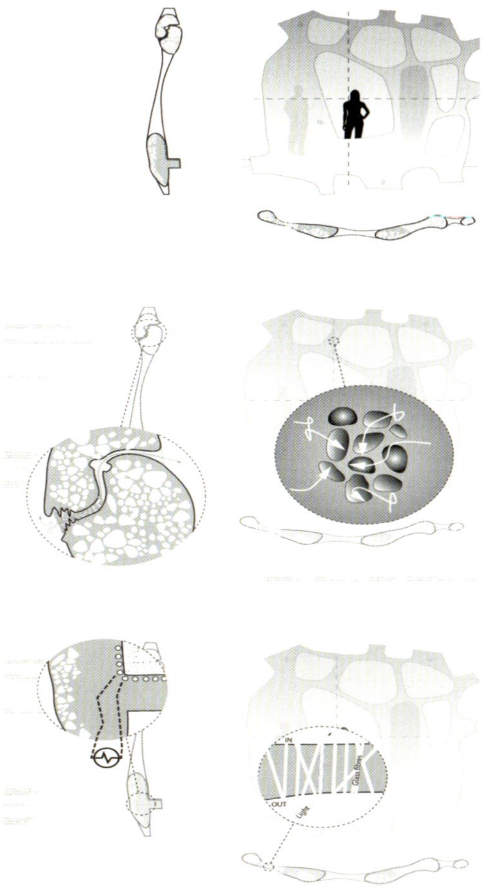

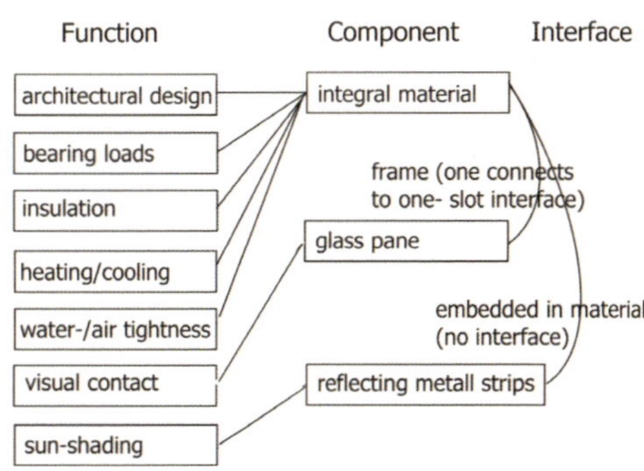
Function
Component
Interface
architectural design
bearing loads
insulation
heating/cooling
water-/air tightness
visual contact
sun-shading
integral material
frame (one connects to one- slot interface)
glass pane
embedded in material (no interface)
reflecting metall strips

# INTEGRATED PERMANENT FORMWORK

30-03-2011

IMAGINED BY Peter van Luijn, guided by M. Bilow and H. Techen
KEYWORDS layered construction, modular, heating, cooling, easy to assemble, envelope, textile, plastics, air
PERFORMANCE integrated functions

The goal of this concept is to integrate building services functions such as heating and cooling into the formwork.
To create the walls, permanent formwork is mounted onto the foundation and stabilized by air pressure. Conventional formwork is not needed or carries stabilizing functions only. The flexible formwork is made from waterproof coated textiles and can be shaped and dimensioned to comprise different chambers with pre-integrated heating and cooling ducts as well as insulation layers. On site, the chambers are filled with concrete and thus become load-bearing elements. The formwork remains in place and serves as the finished surface of the wall element.

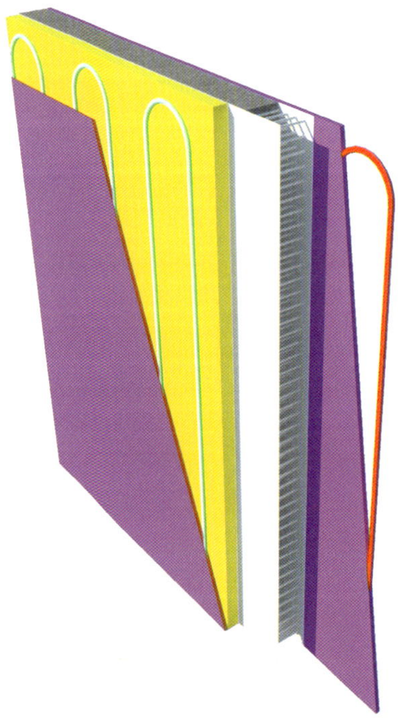

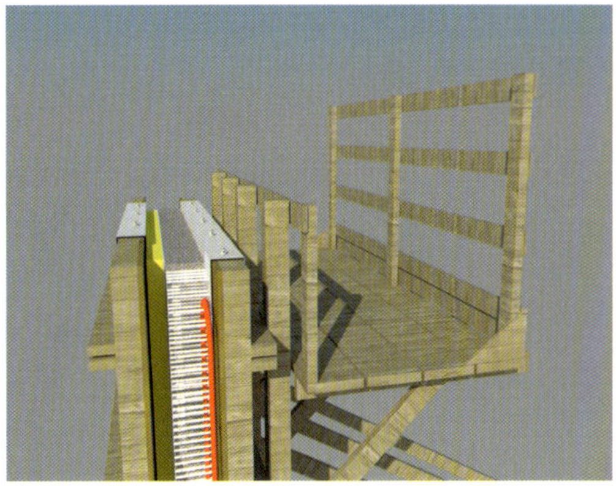

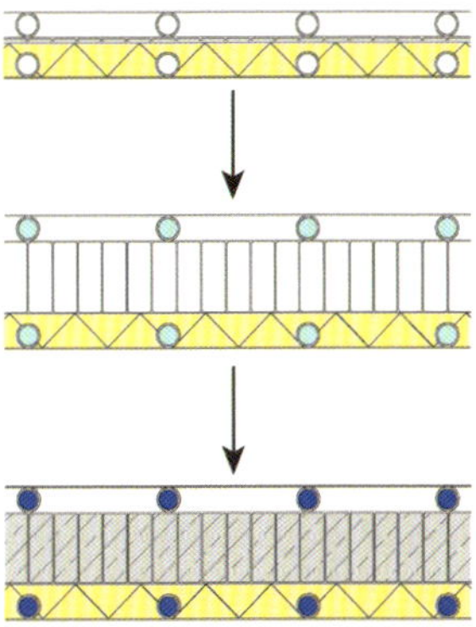

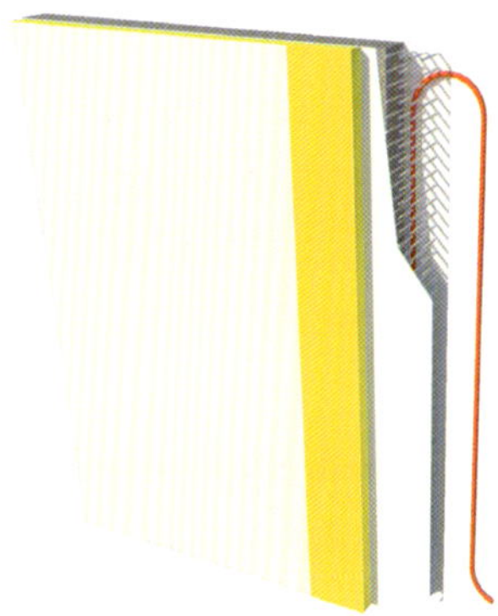

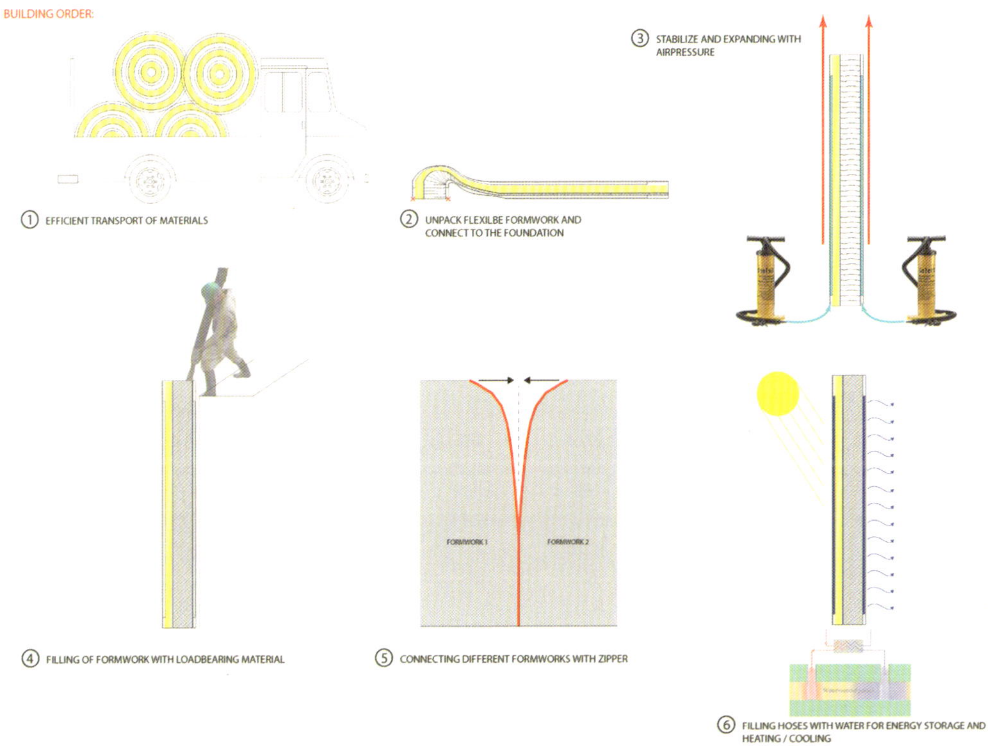
BUILDING ORDER:
① EFFICIENT TRANSPORT OF MATERIALS
② UNPACK FLEXILBE FORMWORK AND CONNECT TO THE FOUNDATION
③ STABILIZE AND EXPANDING WITH AIRPRESSURE
④ FILLING OF FORMWORK WITH LOADBEARING MATERIAL
FORMWORK 1
FORMWORK 2
⑤ CONNECTING DIFFERENT FORMWORKS WITH ZIPPER
⑥ FILLING HOSES WITH WATER FOR ENERGY STORAGE AND HEATING / COOLING

# INTEGRATED SKELETON STRUCTURE

12-03-2011

**IMAGINED BY** Tillmann Klein
**KEYWORDS** latticed girder, integrated insulation and lightning
**PERFORMANCE** integrated functions

Depending on the material selected for the load-bearing frame, the structural system and its geometry provided the basis for setting up an integral façade. Additional functions such as insulation and lighting are added around the load-bearing structure. For this, on-site casting and/or coating is certainly the most innovative approach. Insulation as well as daylight directing should be achieved with materials cast on site.

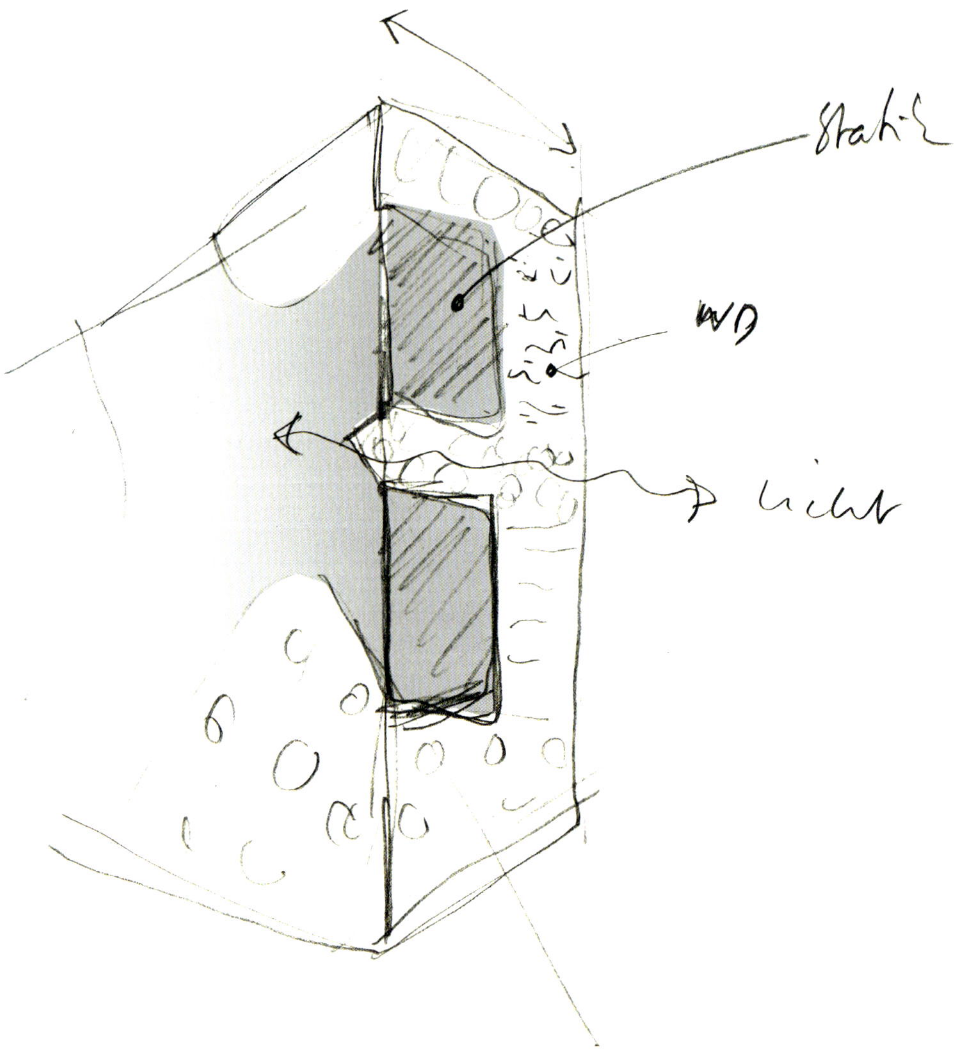

# LAYERED CONSTRUCTION

18-05-2009

**IMAGINED BY** Jasper Overkleeft, guided by T. Klein
**KEYWORDS** layered construction, modular, heating, cooling, easy to assemble, envelope, textile, plastics, air
**PERFORMANCE** integrated functions, premanufacturing of standard components, reusability

Examples such as space suits, Gore-Tex jackets and milk containers prove that the combination of layers with different properties can lead to remarkable performance. A space suit is only a few millimeters thick, but can protect against very low temperatures and dangerous radiation.

In the system presented here, some of the functions are created by combining different components: insulation properties are achieved by a combination of pneumatic cushions and reflective layers. The enveloping foil and the pneumatic cushions (working as structural spacers) in combination with pre-stressing under pressure are used to create stiffness. Flexible warm water capillary tubes are integrated for heating purposes. All layers are only temporarily held in position until they are fixed in place by the application of underpressure. This also means that the interface is created by a combination of components rather than a defined physical interface. Of course, the edge of the façade requires an airtight frame. The arrangement of the layers can be adjusted according to user needs, the architectural idea and the orientation of the building.

From a design viewpoint, many different colors, light emitting foils, etc. could be integrated. The façade could be transparent, translucent or opaque. At a later stage, the layers could also be rearranged to accommodate modified or new façade properties or to add new technologies. This type of façade is lightweight and could be transported in a rolled-up manner. It can be tailored like a sail and formed into 3-D shapes.

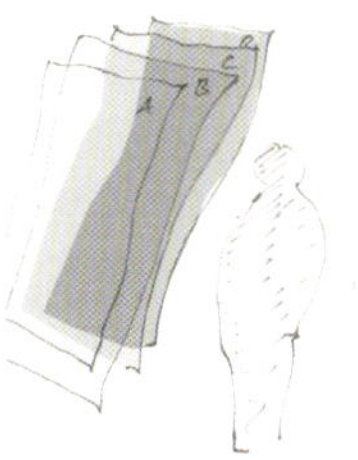

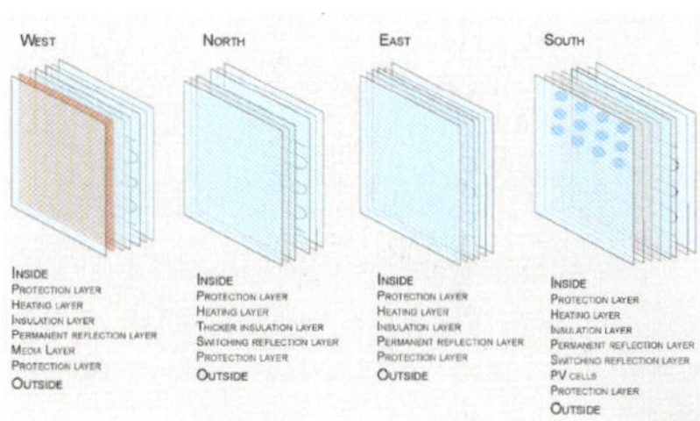


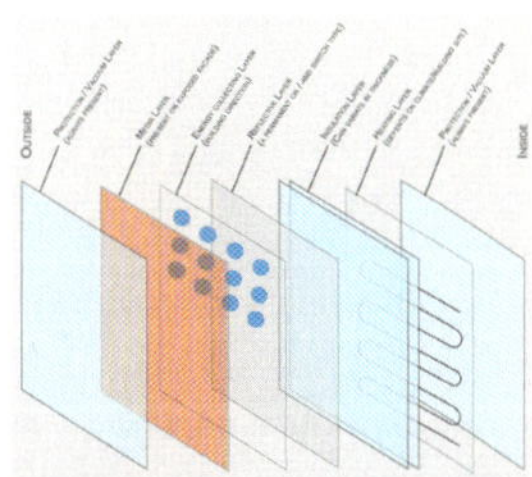


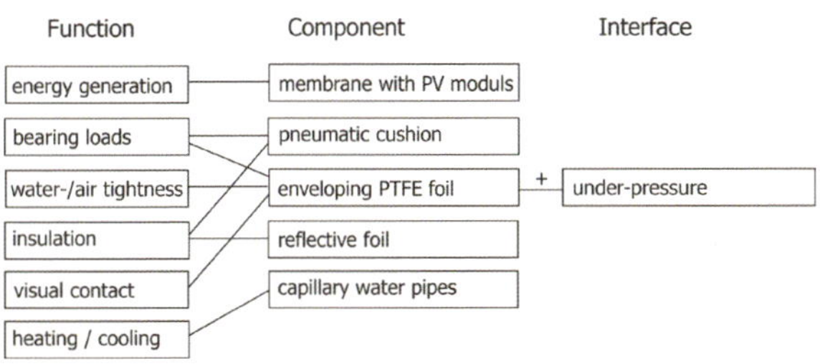


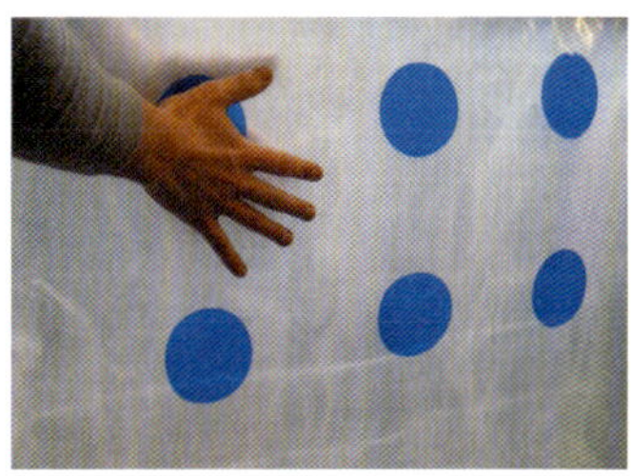

# M&M'S® FAÇADE

30-03-2011

**IMAGINED BY** Sharon Lighart, guided by M. Bilow and H. Techen
**KEYWORDS** layered construction, modular, cooling, easy to assemble, envelope
**PERFORMANCE** integrated functions

Typically, concrete consists of aggregates and cement paste. The aggregate has a significant influence on the performance capability of the final material. The innovative concept presented here can enhance the functions of a wall determined by a particular combination of different aggregates. Depending on the composition, the aggregate or granulate can take on functions such as load-bearing, insulating, and heat storage, amongst others. Bonding the individual components can be done in two ways: by adding an additional binding agent or by activating an already present enclosing binder.

By reversing the M&M'S® principle, the coating can be dissolved to bond the elements to each other. The composition and thickness of the individual layers determine the density of the building material. It is an innovative concept that makes it possible to realize the functions of a wall in layers according to the given requirements, and one that is only activated in the formwork. This ensures easy handling and a fast building progress. Various materials could be used as a binding agent; activated by adding water or other agents or changing temperatures.

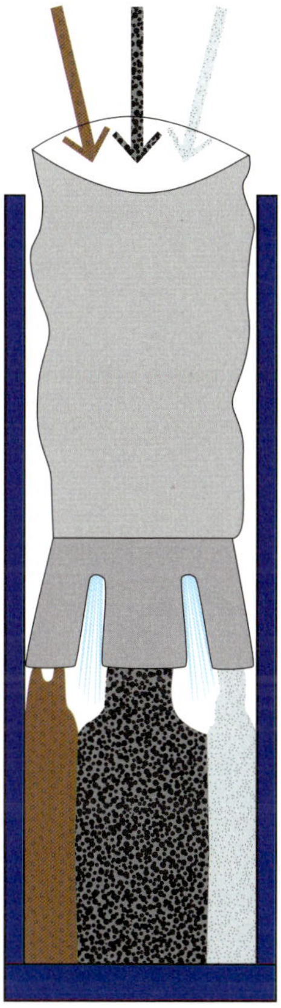

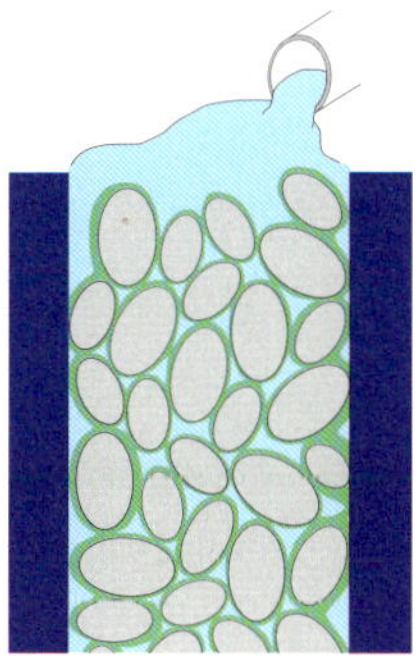

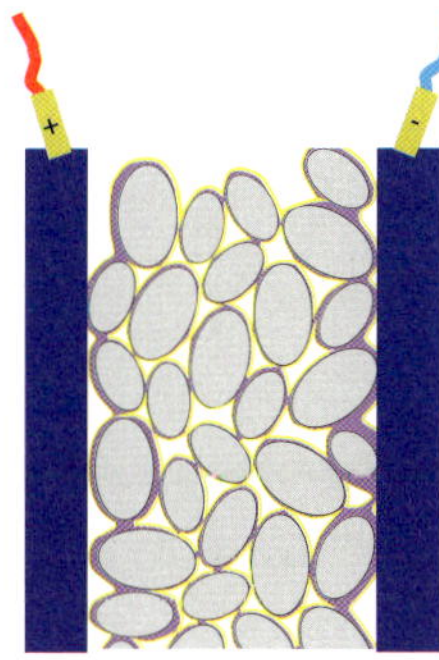

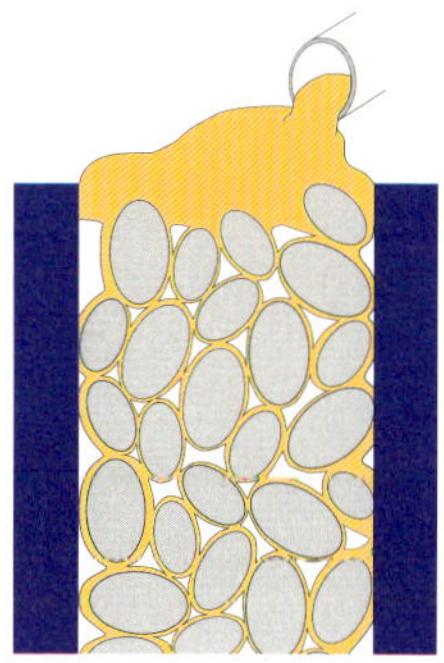

# MATRIX FAÇADE

18-05-2009

**IMAGINED BY** Nathan Volkers, guided by T. Klein
**KEYWORDS** decentralized, modular, ventilating, heating, cooling, adaptive, envelope, aluminum, plastics, membrane, composites
**PERFORMANCE** integrated functions

Interpretation of the grid façade as a media matrix. Future climate integrated façades will be equipped with various installations. Energy, water and information data will need to be transported to all areas of the façade. This is the task of the matrix. It can encompass all different component types. The function structure shows that all transport elements are subcomponents of the matrix and all other components will be attached to the structural frame of the matrix.
A BUS interface is needed to make sure that each component with different properties can be installed anywhere within the matrix and is interchangeable. On top of that, each component is connected to a data cable, water supply line, etc. depending on its functionality. This requires a slot interface. An example for slot interfaces is the motherboard of a computer. A special and unique connection is made for each component such as graphic cards, memory boards, etc.
Local decision making units (DMU) are located at the cross points of the matrix. Together with the central processing unit (CPU), they control all actions. The façade functions as a living organism which constantly adapts to the environment and user needs.
The scale of the matrix depends on the size of the available components. In principle, the grid could be in the range of a couple of millimeters.

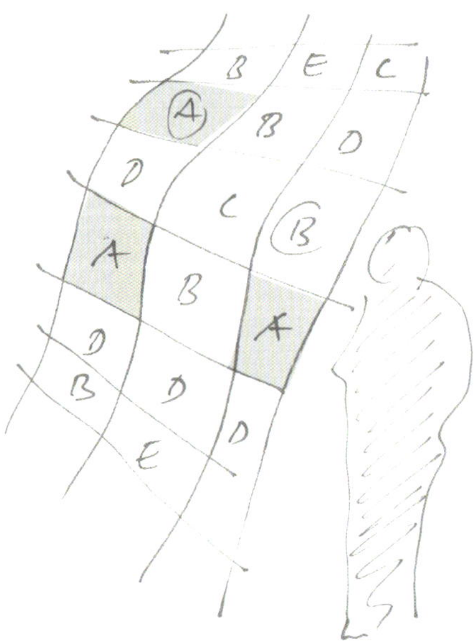

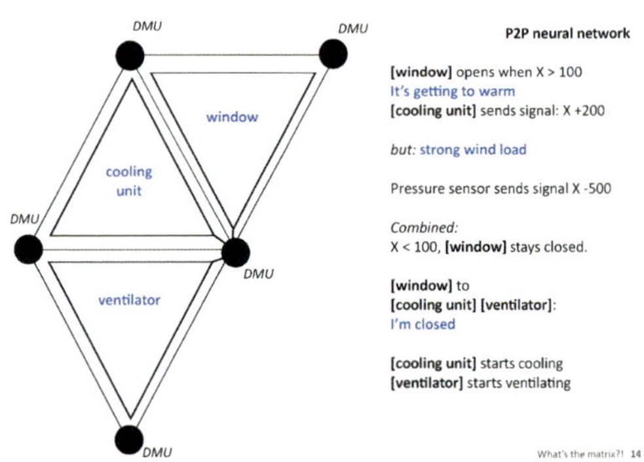

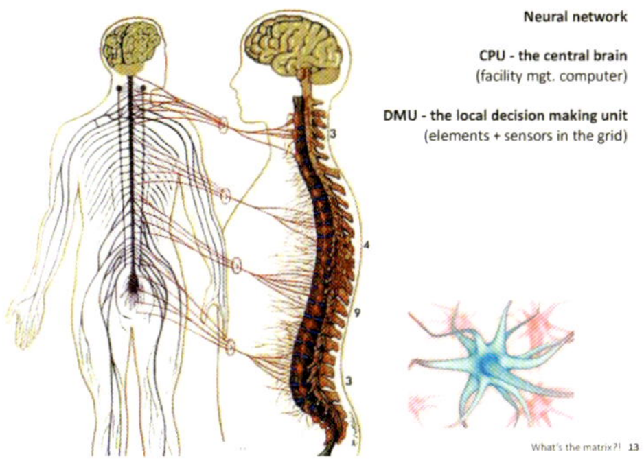
Neural network
CPU - the central brain
(facility mgt. computer)
DMU - the local decision making unit
(elements + sensors in the grid)
What's the matrix?! 13

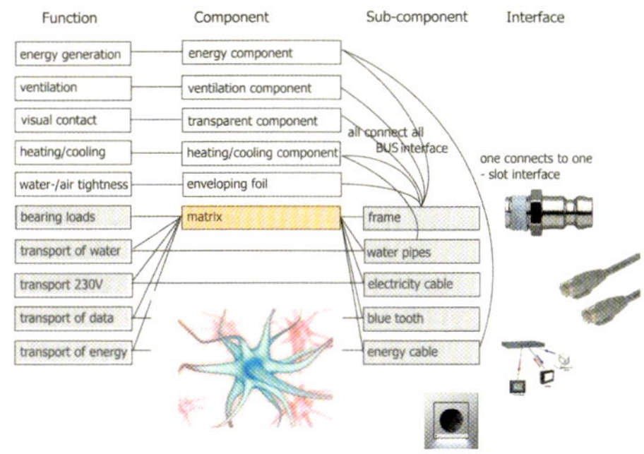
Function
Component
Sub-component
Interface
energy generation
ventilation
visual contact
heating/cooling
water-/air tightness
bearing loads
transport of water
transport 230V
transport of data
transport of energy
energy component
ventilation component
transparent component
heating/cooling component
enveloping foil
matrix
all connect all
BUS interface
frame
water pipes
electricity cable
blue tooth
energy cable
one connects to one
- slot interface

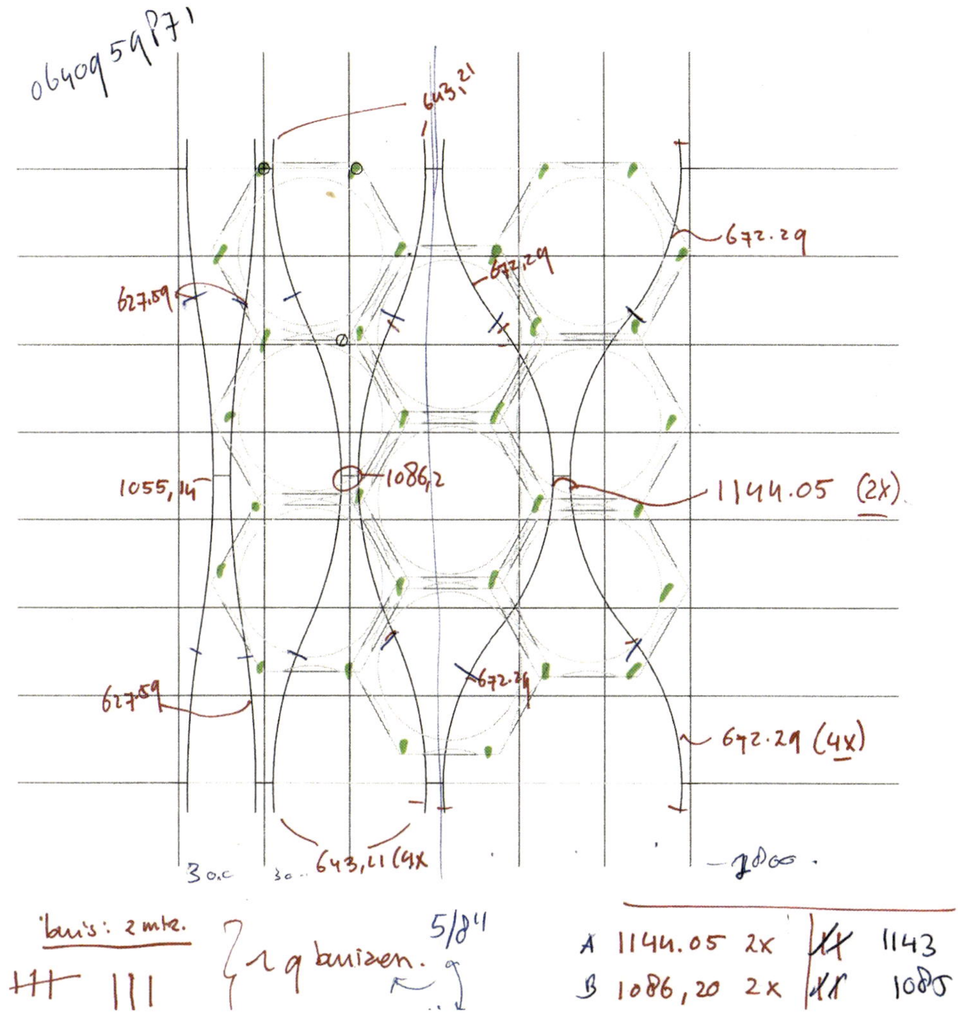
643,21
672.29
627,59
1055,14
1086,2
1144.05 (2x)
672.29 (4x)
643,21 (4x
A 1144.05 2x 1143
B 1086,20 2x 1085

# SMART BRICKS

18-05-2009

IMAGINED BY Willem Kok, guided by M. Bilow
KEYWORDS decentralized, modular, wall, envelope, façade
PERFORMANCE integrated functions

This is a concept for a new wall construction. The elements can be stacked similar to traditional brickwork. The frame of the element carries the loads and can simultaneously accommodate different functions. Such functions could be insulating, energy generation, heating, cooling and other functions serving the interior space. The elements are protected and clad by an arbitrary exterior skin.

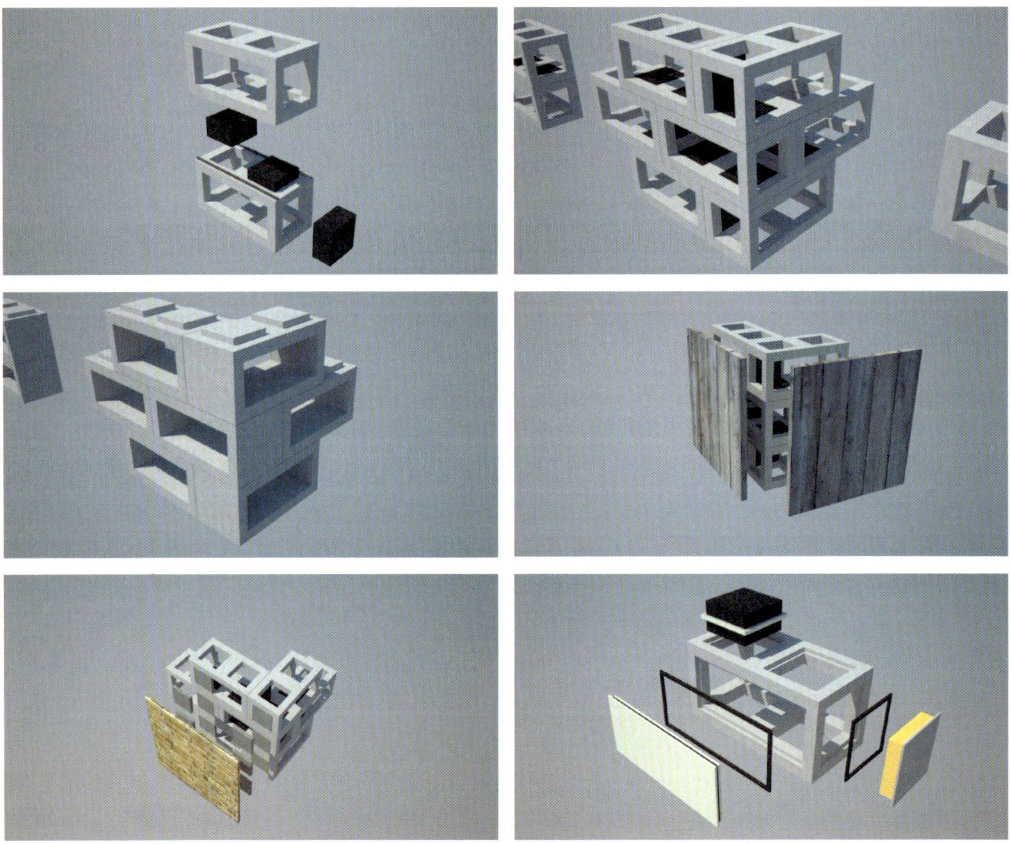

# APPENDIX

# CVs

ULRICH KNAACK (*1964) was trained as an architect at the RWTH Aachen, where he subsequently obtained his PhD in the field of structural use of glass. In subsequent years, he worked as an architect and general planner with RKW Architektur und Städtebau, Düsseldorf, winning several national and international competitions. His projects include high-rise buildings and stadiums. Today, he is Professor of Design and Building Technology at Delft University of Technology, Netherlands, where he established the Façade Research Group and is also responsible for the Industrial Building Education research unit. He has organized interdisciplinary design workshops such as the Highrise XXL. Knaack is also Professor for Design and Construction at the Detmolder Schule für Architektur und Innenarchitektur, Germany, and author of several well-known reference books. He is co-founder of imagine envelope B.V., established in 2008.

TILLMANN KLEIN (*1967) studied architecture at the RWTH Aachen, completing his studies in 1994. He subsequently worked in several architectural offices; from 1996 onward he was employed by Gödde Architekten, focusing on the construction of metal and glass façades and glass roofs. At the same time, he attended the Kunstakademie in Düsseldorf, Klasse Baukunst, completing his studies in 2000 with the title of "Meisterschüler". In 1999, he was co-founder of the architectural office of Rheinflügel Baukunst with a focus on art-related projects. His practical work includes the design of a mobile museum for the Kunsthaus Zug, Switzerland, the design and construction of the façades for the ComIn Business Centre, Essen, project management for the construction of the Alanus Kunsthochschule, Bonn, and project management for the extension of the University of Applied Sciences, Detmold. In 2005, he taught building construction at the Alanus Kunsthochschule, Bonn-Alfter. In that same year he was awarded the Art Prize of Nordrhein-Westphalen for young artists. Since September 2005 he has led the Façade Research Group at Delft University of Technology, Faculty of Architecture. He is co-founder of imagine envelope B.V., established in 2008.

MARCEL BILOW (*1976) studied architecture at the University of Applied Science in Detmold, completing his studies with honours in 2004. During this time, he also worked in several architectural offices, focusing on competitions and later on façade planning. Simultaneously, he and Fabian Rabsch founded the 'raum204' architectural office. After graduating, he worked as a teacher and became leader of research and development at the Chair of Design and Construction at the FH Lippe & Höxter in Detmold under the supervision of Prof. Dr Ulrich Knaack. Since 2005, he has been a member of the Façade Research Group at Delft University of Technology, Faculty of Architecture. He is co-founder of imagine envelope B.V., established in 2008.

HOLGER TECHEN (*1963) studied civil engineering at the Technical University of Darmstadt from 1983 to 1989. Already in his diploma thesis he had analyzed the load-bearing characteristics of glass. This subject has remained his passion. After finishing his studies he started work at the König + Heunisch engineering company in Frankfurt. There he did several dynamics analyses for existing buildings such as chemical and power plants, but focused his work on the application of synthetic fibers in concrete structures. Between 1992 and 1996 he worked on his PhD at the Technical University of Darmstadt in the Institute for Concrete Constructions under Prof. Wörner, again focusing his research on glass constructions. In parallel to his research studies he worked on several glass structures which needed testing in order to reach a final approval for their realization. He finished his PhD thesis "Joining technology for structural glass" in 1997. He continued working on this subject but also in the typical field of a structural engineer at Windels, Timm, Morgen, a well-known Hamburg engineering company. In 2000, armed with his experience of classical structural engineering and his knowledge of glass, he moved back to Frankfurt to start work at Bollinger + Grohmann. There he was project manager on several challenging projects together with famous architects from all over the world. Many of these projects have been published. In September 2006 he was appointed to the chair of structural design and construction design in the architectural department at the Frankfurt University of Applied Sciences. In 2007, together with Matthias Michel, he founded imagine structure, a structural engineering company in Frankfurt.

# REFERENCES

M.F. Ashby, H. Shercliff, D. Cebon: *Materials: Engineering, Science, Processing and Design*, Butterworth Heinemann, Oxford 2007

Aedes: *Ecology.Design.Synergy: Behnisch Architekten + Transsolar Climate Engineering*, Berlin 2006

A. Compagno: *Intelligente Glasfassaden: Material, Anwendung, Gestaltung*, 5th edition, Birkhäuser Verlag, Basle 2002

K. Daniels, D.U. Hindrichs: *Plusminus 20/40 Latitude: Sustainable Building Design in Tropical and Subtropical Regions*, Edition Axel Menges, Stuttgart 2002

M. Davies: "A Wall for All Seasons", in: *RIBA Journal*, 1981, vol. 88, no. 2 (German: "Eine Wand für alle Jahreszeiten", in: *Arch+*, no. 104, 1990)

F. Otto et al.: *Natürliche Konstruktionen*, Stuttgart 1982

U. Pottgiesser: *Fassadenschichtungen Glas*, Bauwerk Verlag, Berlin 2004

T. Herzog, R. Krippner, W. Lang: *Fassaden Atlas*, Birkhäuser Verlag, Basle and Edition Detail, Munich 2004

A. Watts: *Moderne Baukonstruktionen Fassaden*, Springer, Vienna 2004

C. Sauer: *Made of... New Materials Sourcebook for Architecture and Design*, Gestalten Publishers, Berlin 2010

N. Stattmann: *Handbuch Material Technologie*, 2nd, revised edition, ed. Rat für Formgebung, AV Edition, Ludwigsburg 2003

U. Knaack: *Konstruktiver Glasbau*, Rudolf Müller Verlag, Cologne 1998

U. Knaack, W. Führer, J. Wurm: *Konstruktiver Glasbau 2*, Rudolf Müller Verlag, Cologne 2000

U. Knaack, T. Klein, M. Bilow, T. Auer: *Principles of Construction: Façades*, Birkhäuser Verlag, Berlin 2007

C. Schittich (ed.): *Gebäudehüllen: Konzepte, Schichten, Material*, Birkhäuser Verlag, Basle and Edition Detail, Munich 2001

E. Zijlstra: *Material Skills: Evolution of Materials*, Materia, Rotterdam 2005

C. Lüling: *Energizing Architecture: Design and Photovoltaics*, Jovis Verlag 2009

V. Ballard Bell: *Materials for Design*, Princeton Architectural Press 2006

S. Kieran, J. Timberlake: *Refabricating Architecture*, McGraw-Hill Companies 2004

M. Ashby: *Materials Selection in Mechanical Design*, 3rd edition, Elsevier 2005

# CREDITS

## IMAGINE 03 – PERFORMANCE DRIVEN ENVELOPES

Series on technology and material development, Chair of Design of Constructions at Delft University of Technology. Imagine provides architects and designers with ideas and new possibilities for materials, constructions and façades by employing alternative or new technologies. It covers topics geared toward technical developments, environmental needs and aesthetic possibilities.

### SERIES EDITORS
Ulrich Knaack, Tillman Klein, Marcel Bilow

### PEER REVIEW
Martin Haas, BDA/Behnisch Architects, Visiting Professor (Miller Chair), University of Pennsylvania, Philadelphia
Uta Pottgiesser, Hochschule OWL/Detmold
Claudia Lüling, Fachhochschule Frankfurt a.Main

### AUTHORS
Ulrich Knaack, Holger Techen, Tillmann Klein, Marcel Bilow

### TEXT EDITING
Usch Engelmann, John Kirkpatrick

### DESIGN
Studio Minke Themans

### PRINTED BY
Die Keure, Bruges

ISBN 978-90-6450-675-8


www.010.nl

This book is made possible by the support of the following partners: Penn State University, Faculty of Architecture, Eleanor R. Stuckemann Visiting Chair; imagine structure GmbH; imagine envelope b.v.

### ILLUSTRATION CREDITS
All illustrations by the authors and people who contributed to this book, or as mentioned in the image description.

### ALSO PUBLISHED
Imagine 01 – Façades
ISBN 978-90-6450-656-7

Imagine 02 – Deflateables
ISBN 978-90-6450-657-4

Imagine 04 – Rapids
ISBN 978-90-6450-676-5

Imagine 05 – Energy
ISBN 978-90-6450-761-8

### TO BE PUBLISHED
Imagine 06 – Re-Use
Imagine 07 – Bionics